Manston's
Before You Leave
On Your Vacation...

Also in the Travel Key Guide series:

Manston's Flea Markets, Antiques Fairs, and Auctions of Britain

Manston's Flea Markets, Antiques Fairs, and Auctions of France

Manston's Flea Markets, Antiques Fairs, and Auctions of Germany

Manston's Travel Key Europe '88

Manston's Travel Key Britain

The paper in this book meets the ANSI Standard Z39.48-1984 for permanence of paper for printed library material.

Manston's
Before You Leave
On Your Vacation...

How to Protect Your Home, Valuables, Pets, and Plants from Theft and Neglect

Robert C. Bynum and Paula R. Mazuski

A Travel Key Guide
Published by Travel Keys
Sacramento, California, U.S.A.

Published by Travel Keys
in association with Prima Publishing
and distributed by St. Martin's Press

Travel Keys
P. O. Box 160691
Sacramento, California 95816 U.S.A.
Telephone (916) 452-5200

Prima Publishing
P.O. Box 1260
Rocklin, California 95677 U.S.A.
Telephone (916) 624-5718

St. Martin's Press
175 Fifth Ave.
New York, New York 10010 U.S.A.
Telephone (212) 674-5151

Designed by Peter B. Manston
Edited by Peter B. Manston
Printed and bound by Arcata Graphics
Manufactured in the United States of America
First Printing April 1988

Library of Congress Cataloging-in-Publication Data
Manston, Peter B., 1951-
[Before you leave on your vacation]
Manston's before you leave on your vacation : how to protect your home, valuables, pets, and plants from theft and neglect / Robert C. Bynum and Paula R. Mazuski   p.   cm.
"A travel key guide."   Includes index.
ISBN 0-931367-13-1 (pbk.) : $5.95
1. Dwellings—Security measures.   2. Burglary protection. I. Bynum, Robert C., 1924-   . II. Mazuski, Paula R., 1944-   . III. Title. IV. Title: Before you leave on your vacation.
TH9745.D85M36 1988   643'.16—dc19   88-12349 CIP

Contents

Acknowledgements

Thanks to the following individuals and their companies who provided invaluable information and assistance. In no way, however, should they be held responsible for inaccurate or incomplete information in this book; that rests with the authors. American Society for the Prevention of Cruelty to Animals, New York, New York; American Boarding Kennel Association, Colorado Springs, Colorado; Celia Barry, Davis Police Department, Davis, California; Jim Buckingham and Ken Rehg, Davis Lumber Company, Davis, California; Teresa T. Bynum, Davis, California; Canadian Post Corporation, Ottawa, Ontario, Canada; Betsy Cantrell, National Sheriffs' Association, Alexandria, Virginia; Carmen Chambers and Pam Heller, Pacific Gas and Electric Company, Davis, California; Walt Conlan, Discount Alarm Systems, Sacramento, California; Mike Cook, RSA, Sacramento, California; Dan Dickfoss, Liberty Bell Alarm, Sacramento, California; Betty Fletcher, Iron Elegance, Sacramento, California; David Fritz, Gardena Inc., Minnetonka, Minnesota; Martha Griffin, Yolo County Sheriff's Office, Woodland, California; Lynne Haley and Cindy Mabrey, Radio Shack, Ft. Worth, Texas; Patricia Hisey, Sacramento, California; The Home Folks House-Sitting Service, Sacramento, California; Greg Marks, Schlage Lock Company, San Francisco, California; Richard Moffatt, Sacramento Police Department, Sacramento, California; Richard Moore, Jr., Orchard Supply Company, Sacramento, California; National Crime Prevention Council, Washington, D.C.; Scott Necco, Ornamental Iron Outlet, Sacramento, California; Peter Neville, Black & Decker, Shelton, Connecticut; Matt A. Peskin, National Association of Town Watch, Inc., Wynnewood, Pennsylvania; Tom Phister, Allstate Insurance Company, Davis, California; Danielle Poirier and George Watts, Royal Canadian Mounted Police, Ottawa, Canada; Dave Rapelje, Sacramento Home Security Center, Sacramento, California; Dave Rye, X-10 (USA), Northvale, New Jersey; Sharon Tarrance, Pacific Bell, Sacramento, California; The Animal Lover Boarding Kennel, Sacramento, California; Jack Walsh, Burle Industries (formerly RCA New Products Division), Lancaster, Pennsylvania; and Vicki Wright, Sacramento County Sheriff's Department, Sacramento, California.

The following equipment items were requested from and provided by the manufacturers for testing. Each product was installed and performed as advertised and described in catalog material. The authors wish to thank these companies for their cooperation in our efforts to make the book complete.

Black & Decker products
 Professional Home Security System, Model 9105
 Professional Home Security System Outside Siren, Model 9106
Gardena products
 Water Computer 2030, Catalog No. 1162
 Watertimer, Catalog No. 1185
RCA products (Burle Industries, formerly RCA New Products Division)
 RCA Indoor Security Switch, Model C-21
 RCA Outdoor Security Switch, Model C-24
Radio Shack products
 Motion System, Catalog No. 49-0308
 Message Dialer, Catalog No. 49-0431
 Window Alarm, Catalog No. 49-0494
 HomeMinder, Catalog No. 61-2673
 Appliance Module, Catalog No. 61-2681
 Light Dimmer Module, Catalog No. 61-2682
 Universal Appliance Module, Catalog No. 61-2684
Schlage Keepsafer Plus Security System
X-10 (USA) Inc. products
 RS-232 Computer Interface for IBM and Compatibles, Model CP 290/PC
 Lamp Module, Model LM 465
 2-Pin-Appliance Module, Model AM 486
 Wall Switch Module, Model WS 467
 3-Way Wall Switch Module, Model WS 4777
 Companion Switch Module, Model CS 277
 Wall Receptacle Module, Model SR 227
 Battery Backup Timer, Model 75100

In addition to the above, the authors also installed and/or tested deadbolt locks, window locks, various timers, programmable light switches, automatic sprinkler systems, drip irrigation systems, water timers, and low-voltage garden lights systems.

Disclaimer of Responsibility

This book is as complete and accurate as possible. Facts have been exhaustively checked and rechecked. Therefore, though the information and prices are deemed to be accurate, they may differ to some degree from what you find. Neither the authors nor the publisher can be responsible if you are inconvenienced by the information contained in the book.

The persons, companies, and institutions named in the book are believed to be reputable and engaged in the business or service they purport to. Any questions about their products and services should be directed to them rather than the publisher. Inclusion or exclusion of mention of a firm or organization is not a reflection on the suitability of their service or product.

When you find differences, please let us know. What *you* find and suggest can make the next edition even more complete and more useful to future readers.

Introduction

When you leave home, you want to return to find it just as you left it, with everything in its proper place. You want your plants lush after your absence, and your pets happy, healthy, and eager to greet you.

Have you noticed a home in your neighborhood with newspapers lying around the yard, grass unmown, and maybe turning brown from lack of water or an attack of lawn moths? Or have you seen an apartment in your building that has an overflowing mailbox or flyers and throwaway newspapers scattered around the door?

These are sure signs that no one is home, and, even more, signals to a potential burglar.

Burglaries are one of the most common crimes—more than three million are committed each year in the United States and nearly 230 thousand in Canada. Don't let your home become a statistic.

This book will help you ensure that your home, plants, and pets survive your absence, whether for a few days or a few months. You'll find out about—

- home protection systems.
- plant, garden, and pet care.
- safeguarding your family heirlooms and other valuables
- house sitters.
- handling emergencies via long distance.
- contact persons to handle problems while you're away.
- and dozens of other hints to put your mind at ease so you can enjoy your vacation.

You'll create your own "House Book," which lists all kinds of information for anyone taking care of your home or apartment in your absence. They will find—

- the name of your plumber if the plumbing backs up.
- the "house rules" for your house sitter.
- name, address, and phone number of your pet's veterinarian.
- the contact person to be notified in case of a major emergency when you are hundreds or thousands of miles away.

Use the fill-in pages near the end of this book to complete your "House Book." If you have a personal computer, you can keyboard the "House Book" information, making updates easier, and print out sections as you need them.

Much of the information in this book will be useful every day—while you are away for just an hour or two or an evening—as well as for an extended trip.

Prices mentioned throughout this book are list or retail prices, given in United States dollars. Prices will often be different in Canada. Also, many items mentioned are frequently available at discount stores or on sale.

Have a happy and carefree vacation!

Your House Book

What Is a House Book?

A House Book is the information book you create for people taking care of your home while you are away on vacation. It includes facts about your house, family, and possessions that it might be necessary for someone else to know, or for you to know. It contains information for house sitters, baby sitters, pet sitters, and your key contact person about the many routine things that you take for granted. It contains information that you, a member of your family, or another person caring for your home and possessions might need in an emergency.

Everyone can use a House Book, whether you rent or buy, whether you live in a house, mobile home, condominium or apartment. In fact, you probably already have the start of a House Book and don't even know it. You may have a few sheets of paper in a drawer, or a small notebook, or just information in your head. But if it can't be found or is not easy to use, it is of no use in an emergency.

What Goes into a House Book?

The information that goes into a House Book will vary. If you
are using a house sitter, it should be more complete than if you
are merely having somebody check in once in a while. If you
have pets that will be cared for at home while you are gone,
you will need to include information about pet care. You may
need less information if you live in a rented apartment than if
you live in a single—family home with a pool and spa.

Use the "Forms for Your House Book" in the back of the book
to create your own House Book.

Here are some of the things your House Book should
include.

Home Security

Include information about home security:
* Burglar alarms: how to set them and turn them off.
* Lighting controls: how they work and whether they
  need to be reset.
* Doors, windows, and drapes.

See the "Everyday Security Measures" and "Improving
Home Security" chapters.

Valuables

Create an inventory of your valuables. In your House Book in-
dicate that the inventory exists and where it is located. Also
include the name, address, and telephone number of your insurance agent.

See the "Valuables" chapter.

Utilities

Include the location of utility service entries, and how to turn
various utilities off and on:
* Electricity: Where is the service entry, and the switch
  fuse or circuit breaker? How do you turn it off and on?

- Gas: Where is the meter and shutoff valve, and where can the proper tools be found to turn it off?
- Water: Where are the street valve or pump, main valve on the property or apartment, and inside shut-offs? Where is the valve for draining the system (in severe winter areas only). What tools are needed and where are they?
- Sewers and septic tanks: If your home is connected to a sewer system, where is the clean out? If not connected to a sewer system, where is the clean out and where is the septic tank located? Do you have a preferred plumber or septic cleaning company? Write down their addresses and telephone numbers.

Systems and Appliances

Where are the following appliances located and how do you turn them off or on:
- Water heater(s) and water softeners.
- Space heaters and air conditioners.
- Whole house fans.
- Appliances such as refrigerators, dishwashers, microwave ovens, ranges, ovens, washing machines, and dryers.

You should also include the location of operating manuals and instructions for these appliances and systems. It is best to leave all of the manuals are in the same place.

Trash and Garbage

Describe in detail the handling of garbage and trash, including:
- When is trash and garbage picked up?
- Is there a special place that you are required to put it?
- Are there any special preparations, such as separating it, or things to keep out for recycling?
- What is the telephone number for complaints?

Mail, Parcels, and Bills

Where is mail delivered, and where is the nearest post office? If delivery is attempted for packages, where must they be picked up?

Are there letters or payments to be mailed out on a particular date? Clearly identify the letter and the date it is to be mailed. What bills may come in and what, if anything, is to be done with them?

See the "Mail, Newspapers, Other Deliveries, and Bills" chapter.

Newspapers

What newspapers and shopper papers are delivered?

Will the newspapers continue to be delivered when you are away? Whom do you call if not delivered on time?

Do you receive free shopper papers? Should they be saved or thrown away?

See the "Mail, Newspapers, Other Deliveries and Bills" chapter.

Automobiles and Other Vehicles

Include the following information for each vehicle:
- Make and license number. Note which one you take and which you leave.
- Authorized users of each car in your absence and the conditions of its use.
- Name, address, and telephone number of your insurance agent and insurance policy numbers.

See the "Vehicles" chapter.

Pets

Include information about the care and feeding of each of your pets.

See the "Pets" chapter.

Yard and Garden Care

Include information about:
- What to water.
- What lawn care is needed.
- Insect and pest prevention.
- Picking flowers, fruits, and vegetables.

See the "Lawn and Garden" chapter.

Indoor Plants

Include instructions for the care and feeding of house plants.
See the "House Plants" chapter.

House Rules

Include the rules that the house sitter and guests are expected to follow.
See the "House Sitters" chapter.

Telephone Numbers

Record the names and telephone numbers of:
- Persons you want notified if anything happens to you.
- People who can help find you in an emergency.
- Police, and fire departments.
- Utility companies.
- Repair companies you do business with (plumbers, roofers, electricians, etc.)
- Neighbors.
- Veterinarian.
- Physician.
- Relatives.

Itinerary

What are your travel plans? Describe them. If possible, include dates, hotels where you will stay, and the other places where you may be reached. This may help locate you in an emergency.

Insurance Information

List the name, address and telephone number of your insurance agent, and, for each policy, its type, policy number, and company.

Your Will

Do you have a will? Where is it? Where are your burial instructions? (Do not keep your will or burial instructions in a safe deposit box or in an office that is inaccessible after regular business hours.)

What Shouldn't Go into a House Book?

A House Book is something that other people will see. Do not put things into it that could compromise the safety or security of you, your home, or your valuables. For example, don't write down safe combinations, automatic bank teller card numbers, the security codes to your alarm system, or the location of security system switches. Do not put your inventory of valuables into your House Book.

What Will Your House Book Look Like?

You have three choices about how to format your House Book:
  • Use the "Forms for Your House Book" section of this book as your House Book. It provides forms you can fill in about the subjects covered in this book.

- Use a loose leaf binder. A loose leaf binder will be easy to write in and easy to read. If you use a small binder, you can use the forms provided in this book.
- Use your computer. Put the information about your house into a word—processing computer file and update it as things change. When you are ready to go on vacation, print out the information.

Where to Put Your House Book

Once you have completed your House Book, put it in a place that is easily accessible: in a drawer near the telephone, on your desk top, or near some other place that seems logical.

Tell the People Who Need to Know

Now that you have a House Book, how will anybody know about it when they need it?

- Tell your key contact person where it is.
- Tell your pet sitter, house sitter, and baby sitter where it is.
- Tell the person who is most likely to be the first to know if something is going wrong at your house.
- Tell the person who is the most likely to know if something happens to you.
- Tell your best friend.
- Tell the person who has a key to your house.

Key Contact Person

What Is a Key Contact Person?

Your key contact person is the trusted person at home who will:
* coordinate information when emergencies happen.
* periodically check in on your house sitter (if not the same person) to see that things are going according to plan.
* know the burglar alarm code and other details about your security systems that you do not want to put into your House Book.
* know where you are.

Your key contact person has your best interests at heart, has good judgment, and can be counted on when things go wrong and need fixing. You'll have peace of mind knowing that you'll have a key contact person at home.

The key contact person can be the same person as a house sitter. The key contact person can also be the person who feeds your pets and takes care of your plants.

Selecting Your Key Contact Person

When selecting your key contact person, you should consider several factors:

The person should be reliable. You need to be sure that he or she will be there when needed and will carry out plans that have been arranged.

The person should be trustworthy. You must feel confident that he or she will carry out your plan and desires.

The person should be competent. He or she should be able to contact those people that need to be contacted, understand your directions, and know what to do if things do not go according to plan.

The person should have common sense. He or she should be able to carry out a reasonable plan of action.

The person should be available. He or she should be around and available, not someone who has other commitments that mean that he or she will not be readily available.

The person should be willing.

The Role of the Key Contact Person

Once you have selected your key contact person, sit down with him or her and go over the things that you would like to have done. Consider emergencies. See the "Emergencies" chapter.

If you have a house sitter, go over the function the key contact person is to have in relation to the house sitter. See the "House Sitters" chapter.

As you read this book, you can probably see ways in which the key contact person can assist you and set your mind at ease when you travel. Write these things down and discuss them with your key contact person.

Tell People About Your Key Contact

After you have decided on the role and duties of your key contact person, give the person's name, address, and home and work telephone numbers to your family and friends. If you rent, give a copy of the form to your building manager or landlord. Include a statement about the roles that the key contact person will perform. A key contact person form has been provided for your use in "Forms for Your House Book" at the back of this book. Put the completed form in your House Book.

Everyday Protection Measures

How can you ensure that your home will be as safe as possible when you return? By taking precautions and using common sense.

Many of these precautions are just common-sense tips that you should be following every day. They don't cost anything and only take a little time. They may even make you feel more secure when you are home.

Right now let's look at what you can do with what's already in place. Your goal is to prepare your home or apartment so it will look lived in while you are away. It should not appear vacant or unattended.

The "Improving Home Security" chapter following this one discusses many of the ways you can improve the security of your place—through alarm systems, locks, and programmed lighting, among others.

Outside Your Home

Lights

Properly placed lights around the outside of your home can help greatly in discouraging burglars and prowlers. These lights should illuminate the front porch, the back porch or patio, and dark side yards.

Your outside lights should go on at dusk and off when you want—either about midnight or, better yet, at dawn.

The address number should be lit at night and visible from the street for convenience of friends and for police answering emergency calls, whether you're home or not. Either flip the switch every night and morning or use a timer. For details on automatic lighting, see the "Improving Home Security" chapter.

Doors

Keep outside doors locked. Doors should be solid, in frames that aren't easily kicked loose, and equipped with deadbolt locks; you'll find details about deadbolt locks in the "Improving Home Security" chapter.

If your garage is attached to your house, the door leading into the garage should also be locked. Frequently, these are not strong doors and have glass panes, making them easy to enter. In the relative safety of the garage, a burglar has time to open a door into the house.

Keep garage doors locked, preferably with a lock on the inside. Electrically operated doors are not easily opened from the outside without a transmitter. They can easily be opened from inside the garage. Remember that there is a certain number of possible codes—up to a million on some systems—for an electric garage door system, so chances are your code will be the same as someone's, somewhere. Some professional installers leave the code settings as they come from the factory, which increases changes of duplication. Check your installation/operating instructions to see how to tell if your system is still on the factory setting. You may wish to change your code—usually a simple matter of resetting the "dip switch" sequences in both the transmitter and the receiver.

Pet Doors

Pet doors large enough for some dogs can also allow entry by a person. Some clever burglars have a child along to crawl through pet doors and unlock the house. If you do not leave your dog at home, close and lock the opening.

Windows

Lock all windows. Double-hung windows usually have locks. Sliding aluminum windows also have locks, but older ones can sometimes be lifted from their tracks. If you have sliding aluminum windows, try lifting one out of its track. On some, you have to open the window all the way before it will lift out. Simple, inexpensive ways to protect windows are covered in the "Improving Home Security" chapter.

Trees and Shrubs

Prune shrubs to eliminate places for intruders to hide while tampering with windows or doors. Prune trees to prevent burglars' access to upper windows.

Thorny or prickly plants around the house, such as holly, pyracanthas, and roses, add protection to the outside of your home, because they can make it uncomfortable to get close to the house to peek in (see "Improving Home Security").

Vehicle in Driveway

Leave a car in your driveway, parked close enough to the garage door so that no one can open the door. But be sure someone hoses down the car if it gets dusty or dirty, or this will be another clue to a prospective burglar that there is no one at home.

Mail and Newspapers

Don't let mail and newspapers pile up around your front door. See the "Mail, Newspapers, Other Deliveries, and Bills" chapter.

Garbage

Be sure to have someone take care of your garbage containers when you are away. If you leave the containers out for garbage pickup, the containers should be put away when emptied. If pickup will be several days after you leave, have someone put them out on the curb or wherever they are to be emptied, and put away again.

Inside Your Home

Window Shades, Drapes, or Blinds

Tightly drawn window shades, drapes, or blinds during the day are a sure sign there is no one at home. Inside window coverings should be left open, or as you leave them during the day when you are home. If they are at least partially open, neighbors or police can check the inside more easily, particularly at night.

Inside Lights

Lights on timed switches or whole-house control systems can be a deterrent to burglars. Use them. The many types available are discussed in the "Improving Home Security" chapter.

Radios

Everyday sounds from within the house should continue when you are away as much as possible. Radios that come on at certain times and go off at others give the impression, from the outside, that someone is home. This is particularly true if your radios are tuned to talk stations. The same types of timing devices for lamps can turn radios off and on through the evening, just as lights are. If they go on and off at different locations in the house at different times of the day and evening, burglars will have to case the whole house—and will be likelier to leave your home alone.

Radios are preferable to televisions because they are cheaper to operate, and TV sets can sometimes create a fire hazard.

Neighborhood Watch

If your town or city has a Neighborhood Watch Program, Town Watch, Home Alert, or similar program, consider becoming involved. By joining, you and your neighbors help watch each other's property. It makes you and your neighbors more aware of what's going on in your immediate neighborhood.

The Neighborhood Watch Program needs someone on your block or in your building to organize the program and keep track of who lives where. A representative of your local law enforcement agency will outline the program at the first meeting, suggest ways to protect your home, illustrate many security methods with a film or videotape, and give out helpful information on home security, including a check list so you can see just how secure your place is.

Window stickers advertising your part in the Neighborhood Watch Program are also distributed. A sign, often on a power or light pole on your block, will alert passersby (and burglars) that the Neighborhood Watch Program is in effect.

Some police departments will also lend engraving tools for "Operation Identification," so you can put your name, driver licence number, including state or province, on tools, appliances, etc. If something of yours is stolen, it can be identified later at a police station, pawn shop, or in court.

Even if there is no organized Neighborhood Watch Program in your area, you and a neighbor or two can probably work out a mutual help system to keep an eye on each other's places when someone is away.

In the United States, the National Neighborhood Watch Program is part of a national program organized in 1972 by local law enforcement agencies in cooperation with the National Sheriffs' Association. For details, contact:

National Sheriffs' Association
1450 Duke Street
Alexandria, Virginia 22312
Telephone (703) 836-7827

The National Association of Town Watch, Inc., was formed in 1981 to help promote neighborhood action against crime, and includes citizen crime watch groups, law enforcement agencies, and crime prevention organizations. It also publishes a newsletter and sponsors the "National Night Out Against Crime." For details, contact:

National Association of Town Watch, Inc.
7 Wynnewood Road, Suite 215
P.O. Box 303
Wynnewood, Pennsylvania 19096
Telephone (215) 649-7055

In Canada, check with your city or provincial police department or the nearest Royal Canadian Mounted Police office for the closest Neighbourhood Watch program.

Improving Home Security

Discouraging prowlers and burglars isn't easy. Securing your home against break-in is even more difficult. It requires planning and costs at least a few dollars. Just how far you want to go depends on how valuable your belongings are, the crime level in your neighborhood, how much effort you want to go to, and how much money you want to, or can, spend. (Everyday tips for home security were covered in the previous chapter.)

This chapter describes protective devices; you either install them yourself or have someone else install them. There are numerous choices on the market. You must select the types of devices and systems you feel most comfortable with—and decide just how "high tech" you want to go. Some devices plug into wall outlets, others are wireless; still others take advantage of computers and televisions.

You can find home protection devices and systems at hardware and home supply stores, some department stores, electronic and computer supply stores, and even in mail-order catalogues. Browse the hardware and electrical sections of stores for dozens of security items—many of them very inexpensive. Watch the ads in your local newspapers and electronic magazines for sales of such high-cost items as lighting fixtures, light switches, and burglar alarm kits. Look in the Yellow Pages of your telephone book under "Burglar Alarm Systems" and "Security," as well as "Gates," "Guards, Doors and Windows," "Iron Ornamental Work," "Locks & Locksmiths," and "Locks, Wholesale and Manufacturers," for many of the products discussed in this chapter.

The home security items discussed below will give you some idea of the wide range available. You no doubt will find other items of interest.

While the protective measures discussed here are designed to make your home safer, they can frequently provide greater convenience when you are home. You may want to consider some of them for that reason alone.

Whatever measures you choose, your daily life may change somewhat. If you install an interior alarm system, make allowances for your pet roaming around the house at night so it doesn't set off the alarm—or your occasional wandering through the house or downstairs after the alarm is set. Also, you can't just dash in when returning home to answer a ringing telephone if the alarm is set—or you will have an alarm sounding while you answer the telephone.

Lights and Timers

Outside Lighting

Outside lights deter those thinking of entering your home uninvited. They provide more light than most burglars like to work in.

Outside lights should illuminate the front door, back door or yard, dark side yards, and the street address. They can also be incorporated into your landscaping design to add to the beauty of your home.

Garden lights can give a soft glow or occasional spotlit effects that are both attractive and functional. They can highlight steps or a path that is hard to follow in the dark.

Low-voltage (12-volt) lighting systems can be installed easily and do not usually require building permits or installation by licensed contractors. No deep trenching is necessary for the wires, which are strung beneath shrubs or just an inch or two below ground level. The lights are easy to attach to the connecting cable—even when the current is on, so you can see if a connection is working. The control units plug into any outside 110-volt outlet. Basic kits of four to six lights cost about $30 to $40. The systems have timers built into the transformer boxes, so you can set the lights to turn on and off when you want, and then forget about it. Additional lights of various types will add to the cost.

You may find it practical to have your outside porch, flood, and area lights as well as some inside lights controlled automatically so they will go on and off when you are away, as well as when you are home.

Most of the timers and switches for light control are readily available at hardware and home supply stores, electronic supply houses, mail-order firms, and some supermarkets.

Most timers and switches are designed to control incandescent lights only—not fluorescent.

The types of units available are usually one or a combination of the following:

• Simple mechanical timers.
• Digital units you program like a wrist watch.
• Devices that respond to
   a. light intensity.
   b. sound.
   c. movement.
• Devices that sense a combination of light intensity, sound, and movement.
• Computer-programmed units using your personal computer.
• Programmed units using your TV screen.

Some units are simply plugged into electrical outlets, and then lamps or radios plugged into the units and set to go off and on when desired. Other units are wired-in to replace wall switches or electrical outlets. More sophisticated systems control lights and appliances from a console using the electrical wiring throughout your whole house or apartment, or even from your car as you approach, or by remote control through any touch-tone telephone.

Light Switches

Two types of light switches control lights. One is programmed to go on and off at set times. The other type responds to light intensity, sound levels, or movement, or a combination of these.

Programmable Switches

Programmable light switches (from $15 to $30 each) are easy to install by replacing existing switches. You might want to read the features described on the package or carton to see which you like best. Some simply turn the lights on and off at a set time, or sequence of times, and others can turn the lights on at a predetermined dim setting as well as on or off, once or several times in a 24-hour period.

Most are as easy to program as a digital wrist watch. Some require more effort than others. Occasionally you find some that seem impossibly complex to program. Read the programming directions before you buy.

You can override programmable switches and timers if the occasion arises, usually by pressing the control button or panel on the switch. Directions come with the unit.

As the seasons change, you should change the program, just as you change your watch, clocks, and timers when daylight saving begins or ends.

One major problem with most digital programmable switches is that they lose their memory in case of a power outage; few have a battery backup. When the power returns, some switches leave the lights off, and some turn them on, depending on the type of circuitry. In these cases, a neighbor or home sitter can reprogram them if the directions are handy and understandable.

Read the directions fully and slowly before you begin to install switches. Turn off the power supply at the service entry before you start!

Light-Sensitive Switches

Light-sensing switches, which cost from $5 to $15, are activated by light intensity levels, turning lights on at dusk and off at dawn. Some turn lights on at dusk and can be programed to turn lights off at a certain time.

Light-sensitive switches can control both inside and outside lights, and an inside switch can control outside lights.

With some light-sensitive switches, you are somewhat at the mercy of the sunlight's intensity, and on some overcast, dark, or stormy days the lights may remain on all day long. Also, light from a nearby source (such as a bright street light) may confuse the sensor. Many, however, are adjustable to light levels that activate them and will respond to the level of darkness you choose.

Plug-in light-sensitive units are also available (about $25) for lamps, turning the light on at dusk and off when you program it to.

Sound-Sensitive Switches

Some switches are activated by sounds, and often work in conjunction with light intensity, so the light works only when it's dark. Noise such as footsteps, doors closing, and breaking glass turns the lights on. You can program how long you want them to stay on. The noise sensors are adjustable for soft-to-loud sound levels. Sometimes outside sounds, such as screeching of tires on the street, can turn on lights. The units cost from $15 to $25.

Plug-in units for lamps are also available for about $25.

Motion-Sensitive Switches

Some switches respond to movement to turn lights on, and can be used both outside and inside. Since they are also adjustable to light levels, they can be set to turn on between dusk and dawn. When someone crosses the switch's infrared beam, the light turns on. You set the length of time you choose it to stay on, from less than a minute up to several minutes. Some of the outdoor sensors can "see" a person up to 75 feet away and an automobile up to 200 feet away. These units also can be turned on and off, if you wish, by flipping the on/off switch that controls the light fixture, thus overriding the motion-sensor feature.

You can purchase just a switch (about $35 to $45) to wire into an existing outdoor incandescent, halogen, quartz, or fluorescent light fixture or purchase a fixture complete with the sensor attached (from $35 to $55). When installing a switch into your own fixture, check the wattage capacity of the switch and compare it with the fixture you wish it to control. If your fixture calls for higher wattage than the switch can supply, you can damage the switch.

The same principle is used in indoor units ($35) that plug into wall outlets. Incandescent lamps plugged into them turn on when you go into a dark room, hall, or basement and remain on for up to several minutes.

Movement-sensitive switches ($35) are also available to plug into a wall-switch replacement for an indoor incandescent light fixture to light your entry into dark rooms, stairways, or other areas. They can stay on as long as 15 minutes; you set the length of time when you install them.

Movement-sensitive units have certain advantages in addition to security. They can turn on when you approach your house or when you go into a dark area, in or outside. Also, they only turn on when something triggers them, so you are not burning lights all night long, unless you wish to do so. They also can turn off a light after the last person has left an area, so no one has to stay behind to turn off the light and leave in the dark. The indoor switches are designed to operate incandescent lights from 25 to 300 watts only, and are not designed to operate TVs, radios, appliances, or fluorescent lights.

Light-Sensitive Controls

You can put inexpensive screw-in light-sensing sockets in light fixtures and lamps in areas where the daylight is bright enough to keep the lights off during the day and turn them on in the evening. These cost about $5 to $8 for indoor units and $6 to $11 for indoor-outdoor units.

These units are not adjustable for light levels, but you can usually turn the sensor "eye" toward the light. If placed in a porch light or lamppost light, they must be in fixtures with clear glass or plastic. Frosted or colored glass or plastic may not let enough light through to the sensor to turn off the bulb during the day. Also, if light from another source strikes the sensor's eye, the sensor may not turn on the light it is controlling, or it may make the light flicker.

Plug-in Units

Mechanical Timers

Plug-in programmable timers for individual wall outlets are widely available, easy to set, and do not lose their memory when power goes off. But their time clocks will have to be reset after a power outage. Available at discount, hardware, and home supply stores, and supermarkets, these timers range in price from $8 to $18, depending on the power capacity and number of on-off settings possible. Usually they are rated at 15 amps, 1250 watts tungsten. Timers are frequently on sale. Do NOT plug a television set into a timer unless it has enough capacity; this can be a fire hazard.

These units often become noisy in time, as their little electric motors begin to wear. Replacement motors are available, if you want to take the time to install it.

Light- and Sound-Sensitive Units

Plug-in units for lamps are available that respond to light levels and sound, just like those discussed above, and are available from $15 to $25.

Memory Units

Plug-in units for lamps are available ($12 to $15) that "memorize" the pattern of usage of a lamp plugged into one and then turns the light on and off automatically.

Central Control Systems

Central control systems that plug into wall outlets and send signals through your house or apartment electrical current are available from several electronic supply, mail order, and home appliance stores. The control units usually have a battery backup so power outages do not interfere with their day-to-day operations. They can control light switches, outlets for lamps and appliances, even thermostats for heating and air conditioning. Some have optional portable transmitters, similar to those that open or close a garage door, to control lights as you drive up to your home. With some, you can call your home on a telephone and signal the lights, appliances, and heating/air conditioning to turn on for your arrival.

You can set each switch, lamp, or appliance unit to go on and off when you wish, including a "security" setting that varies the on/off times each day within an hour of the set time. You can choose daily, weekday, or weekend settings for the cycles. Most of these allow you to turn all the house lights on at once from the central console. Some control units also have the capacity to dim lights.

Control consoles range from $25 to $50; individual "modules" to replace switches or receptacles cost about $12 to $25. Appliance modules that plug into wall outlets cost about $12 to $15. The plug-in modules don't make the constant grinding noise that mechanical timers do when their motors are worn, but you hear a "click" when the units turn on.

You can control an individual lamp or light by turning it on or off once or twice in rapid succession, temporarily overriding the set program. On the next cycle, the program takes over.

Computer and TV Controlled Systems

If you own a personal computer, you can buy whole-house systems that you program through your IBM, IBM-compatible, Apple, Macintosh, or Commodore computer. The control interface (about $50) has a battery backup, so the control unit can be unplugged from the computer and plugged into the house current wherever you want it. It then takes over, sending information signals out to each individual module ($15 to $25) you installed to replace plugs and switches in various rooms. Appliance modules ($15) can handle coffee makers, TVs, and other appliances. The computer capability allows much more flexibility of programming: you can cause each event to occur daily, certain days of the week, and weekends; to turn on and off at set times or at "security" (variable) settings; and have seasonal programs for summer and winter. They even print out the program to include in your "House Book." Burglar-alarm capability can also be added.

Additional control units are available for $12 to $25. Optional radio transmitter and receiving units can turn on lights and appliances as you drive up the driveway; you can also get units to operate your system by transmitting command signals over the telephone.

These systems are available at electronic and computer supply stores.

Another light/appliance control choice ($60) is one that you can program on your television screen. The TV's power cord and antenna plug into the control unit, which sits on or beneath your TV set. A wireless remote like the one that comes with your TV or VCR lets you program on your TV screen, room by room, module by module ($15 to $25 each). You can set on/off programs for time of day, including "security" settings, plus patterns for weekdays, weekends, and certain days, as well as dim and full power, for lighting and appliances. You can turn all the lights on or off at once, if you wish. An individual lamp or light switch, even though programmed, can be individually controlled by turning it on or off once or twice in rapid succession, to override the program in the module. The TV-set program continues in that particular unit when the next cycle comes around. These units are available at electronic supply houses.

Programming Hints

In general, when programming lights, you should have them turn on or off through the house or apartment to reflect your usual "at home" patterns: living-dining area earlier in the evening, bedroom later. The same patterns should be followed if you have radios on timers. If you plug a television into a timer, be sure the timer has the proper power capacity to prevent a fire hazard. Check the capacity of the timer and the power requirement of the TV set (look on the back of your TV set or in its operating manual).

Doors

Hinged Doors

Outside doors should be solid core or steel, in frames that aren't easily kicked loose, and equipped with deadbolt locks. The doors should be hung so that hinge pins cannot be removed from the outside. Tamper-proof hinge screws, available at hardware stores, are recommended if screws are exposed.

You may also want to cover any glass areas with protective coverings—plastic, metal grille, etc.—so that an intruder can't break through the glass and reach in to open a door from the inside.

Deadbolt locks (from $7 up) for your outside doors are highly recommended by the police. One type has a thumb turn on the inside and the other has double cylinders requiring a key inside as well as out to unlock it. The latter offer better protection against intruders, particularly if there is a window near the door that can be broken, enabling a burglar to reach around to open the door with the thumb turn. However, you must remember to keep a key inside when you're home or you can't open the locked door if you need to leave fast in case of a fire or some other emergency.

Screws into the strike plate should be long enough (at least 2 inches, 5.1 cm) to go into the framing.

Some hardware stores have kits with templates and drill bits you can rent to install deadbolt locks.

You can also get kits to reinforce hollow-core doors and strike plates so they aren't easily kicked in.

Install door viewers in solid doors so you can see who's outside without having to open the door.

If you have a mail slot, it should be low enough that no one can look into the house or apartment. If the slot is too high, mail-slot shields are available to install inside the door, but they should allow magazines and other oversize mail to be pushed through the slot.

Sliding Doors

Sliding doors should have catches that can't be wiggled loose or that prevent the doors from being lifted out of their tracks. There is a wide variety of security items available for sliding doors; many of the devices also work on sliding aluminum windows, discussed below.

You can get deadlocks (about $5 to $6 each) that are operated with a key from the outside.

If the standard catch lock on your slider can be wiggled loose, you can keep the door from being opened in several ways:

- Put a length of dowel or broomstick in the track.
- Put a plastic-tubing alarm containing a "screamer" cartridge that fits into sliding door track, emitting a loud screaming noise when the door is tampered with. The units ($20 to $25) fit a door opening up to about 4-1/2 feet, or 1.37 m; replacement screamers are less than $5.
- Drill a hole through in the inside track and part way through the door and put a large-headed heavy nail in the hole to keep the door from being opened or lifted out of its track. You can drill a second hole a few inches back and put the nail in it so you can safely leave the door open a little for ventilation.
- Install an inexpensive pin ($1.50) to use instead of a nail, or use a heavier pin unit that is screwed into the top track; the latter requires a larger hole in the door

frame for the pin, but is always in place and not likely to fall out and get lost.

Door Security

Grilles

Metal grille-work security doors may be necessary if you live in a high-crime area. You can get security doors for as little as $50 (on sale) and install them yourself or have it done. Security doors with screens for a single door cost about $230 plus $50 to $100 installation. Security storm doors cost about $150 to $175 more plus about $65 to $75 for installation. For patio doors, you can get swinging or sliding security doors for about $400 plus about $100 for installation.

Shutters

Roll-down shutters, made of either aluminum or PVC vinyl, are available for outside doors. In addition to providing security, they can cut down on the sun's rays in the summer and cold in the winter. They also can provide ventilation even when closed. An aluminum rolling shutter for a patio door costs about $1400, installed; PVC vinyl runs about 20% less.

Window Security

Security for your windows depends on the type—double-hung wood or metal, aluminum sliding, or louvered (jalousie).

Whether you want to keep your windows partly open when you are away or at night when you are home will also dictate the types of devices you choose.

Double-Hung Windows

Double-hung windows usually come with locks that twist to open or close. You can increase security the of these windows with keyed sash locks ($4 each). Older windows, especially if wood-framed, do not have any way to keep them open just a little for ventilation. You can drill holes through the inside frame to (not through) the outside frame and insert a long nail (1-1/2" to 2", 3.8 cm to 5.1 cm) that will hold the window in place when partly open. Or, you can buy inexpensive vent locks (about $1.60 or so a pair) for opening windows partly for ventilation. Newer, metal-framed double-hung windows have built- in stops to keep them open only a few inches.

Sliding Windows

There are numerous devices to secure sliding windows:
  • A dowel or length of broomstick in the track to keep the window from being opened.
  • A nail or metal pin through the frame and window to keep the window from being opened or jiggled out of its track. Drill a hole through the inside frame and part way into the window frame and insert a large-headed heavy nail (not all the way through to the outside so a burglar can knock it back into the room) or buy pins ($1 to $2 each) at your local hardware or home supply store.
  • A screamer alarm, discussed above under "Doors."
  • Any one of several types of slide stops or locks. Some have set screws ($2 each) and others have keyed locks ($4 to $5) to keep the window closed or partly opened for ventilation with security.

Protective Grilles and Guards

Window protection can be elaborate, from roll-down shutters used widely in some parts of Europe for sun control and security, to decorative grille work. Either of these is recommended for high-crime areas or larger cities. Shutters can be rolled up to clear windows for an unobstructed view, while grille guards are always visible.

Roll-down Window Shutters

The outside aluminum or PVC vinyl roll-down shades provide maximum protection as well as extra insulation against wind, heat and cold, and keep out unwanted sun, particularly on western exposures. They also can be adjusted to allow breezes to flow through the narrow slit-like openings—very helpful in keeping a house or apartment from getting stuffy in the summer. Aluminum shutters cost about $800 for a 3' x 6', 91.5 cm x 183 cm, window, including installation, which can be complicated; PVC vinyl costs about 20% less.

Grille Guards

Grille-work window guards are easier to install than roll-down shades and are cheaper—about $40 to $50 plus about $12 to $15 for installation for a 3' x 6', 91.5 cm x 183 cm, window. When installed, no screw heads should be exposed on the outside; use one-way lag bolts or fasten the guards from the inside. Guards are always visible and do make window cleaning more difficult, but you trade that for security.

If you are planning to use grille guards in bedrooms, be sure the window guards have quick releases (about $75 additional cost per window) in case of fire or other emergency. (This also makes window cleaning easier.)

For less permanent but secure installations, you can buy removable guard kits to allow you to insert the grillwork in brackets when you are going away for a period and then remove them on your return. Or use them in a mountain or beach home for security during the off season.

Louvered Windows

Louvered (jalousie) windows are very easily slipped out of their metal frames unless the panes are glued into place. The edges of the panes should be sanded before epoxy glue is applied to be sure the glue will set and hold.

Alarm Systems—Electronic Watchdogs

Alarm systems can offer protection either when you are away or when you at home if an intruder attempts to break into your place.

Numerous ideas for alarms have been tried to make it appear that someone is at home, particularly with tape recorders that are initiated by the doorbell to give a message or reproduce the sound of a barking dog. These are for the electronics buff to play with, but by themselves usually do not stop a dedicated burglar.

Most individuals really concerned with break-ins install some kind of alarm device. These range run from simple to complex, including:

- Individual sensor units that sound when a window or door is opened.
- Units that detect movement within a single room or area with heat and motion sensors.
- Units that detect noise—breaking glass, doors forced open, etc.
- Sophisticated whole-house systems are turned on and off from electronic key pads or consoles.

Some units make certain lamps flash as well as sound alarms. Message telephone dialers can be added for a "monitored" system that sends a taped telephone message to a security office, or, in some cases, the police department, which will send out someone to investigate.

You must decide if you are interested only in the perimeter of your house—windows, doors, etc.—or if you also want devices for inside detection after someone gets in. You may only choose inside detectors with no perimeter sensors, or you may choose a combination. And you may want a monitored system, at an extra cost per month of $12 to $25, in which a tripped alarm alerts a monitoring service that dispatches the appropriate agency to your home. If the system is connected directly to the police department, you may have to apply for a permit, pay a regular fee, or pay for each false alarm.

Simple Sensors

The simplest units (less than $5) are self-contained sensors about the size of a cigarette package that attach to windows or doors with screws or double-sided pressure tape and contain AA batteries. Each unit sounds its internal alarm if the window or door is opened.

For about $10 you can get key-operated electronic window or door alarms that are about the same size that run on 9-volt batteries. Each has its shrill alarm that sound if the window or door is opened, and has the added feature of a time delay so you can set it (with the key) and leave or come in and turn it off before the alarm sounds.

These are available from electronic supply and mail-order houses.

Area Motion Detector Alarms

Portable alarm units that detect motion in a room and cost less then $100 are available through electronic supply houses and some home supply and hardware stores. They detect movement in a room or area and sound an alarm. You can adjust the placement of these units to keep pets and moving drapes from setting off the alarms.

You can add remote switches to arm and disarm the unit, window and door sensors with tiny transmitters, smoke alarms, and automatic dialers, all tied into central control consoles, to some of these portable alarm units for a do-it-yourself whole-house system. (See Wireless Systems, below.)

Noise Detector Alarms

Portable units with battery backup that hear glass breaking, wood crunching, etc. in a room cost about $250. They contain an alarm and can screen out normal sounds, such as voices, music, and dogs barking.

Whole-House Alarm Systems

Whole-house alarm systems can be either wireless or hardwired (wiring permanently installed in your house) to sound an alarm if someone attempts to break in and, if you choose, to alert a monitoring agency of the attempted break-in. Whole-house systems usually have some or all the type of units discussed above, and may include:

- Sensors—magnetically operated switches—at some or all of the outside doors and windows.
- Glass breakage detectors to respond to the sound of glass breaking.
- Vibration detectors to "hear" doors and windows opening.
- Monitors—usually infrared—to detect motion inside some area of the house.
- Pressure pads under rugs at selective areas of your home—inside the front door, close to cabinets containing particularly valuable items, etc., or a combination of these.
- A central control unit.
- A digital key pad arming/disarming device in which you punch in your own code to turn the alarm on or off. There is a time delay to permit you to enter and leave the house before the alarm sounds.

You can locate companies that install whole-house systems under "Burglar Alarm Systems" and "Security" in the Yellow Pages of your telephone directory.

Some systems can be set to monitor certain areas or "zones" in your home as well and can sound when windows or doors are tampered with at night when you are home. You can still walk around and the motion detector won't work. Some systems can monitor opening or closing of doors (when children go in and out during the day, for instance) and send out a different sound from the alarm system.

Fire protection capability—smoke detectors tied to the alarm system—can be an option.

Some communities require an alarm permit when an alarm system is installed. They also may have regulations on the type of sound alarms emit and length of time an alarm sounds. Some may allow connections to the police department (and may charge for each false alarm), while other departments prohibit direct connection. Check with your local law enforcement office for details.

Wireless Systems

Wireless systems basically consist of a central control console that plugs into a wall outlet (with a battery backup) and magnetic-operated transmitter sensors (also containing batteries) at doors and windows you wish to protect.

Wireless systems are quicker and easier to install than hard- wired systems, and are especially attractive to renters, who can take the system with them when they move. But the parts are more visible, particularly the cigarette-pack-size sensors at windows or doors. The central console with arming touch pad is about the size of a telephone-answering machine. And they can cost more than a hard-wired installed system.

Individual parts for a wireless system cost more than those for a hard-wired system, because the sensors contain tiny radio transmitters and batteries. Installation costs for wireless systems is much less than for hard-wired systems. Kits with two or three sensors cost about $140 to $150, with extra sensors and various options available. A system for a typical suburban home of three bedrooms can cost about $900 to $1,100 installed by a professional, and about $200 less if you do it yourself. Monitoring by a security company costs about $12 to $25 a month.

You have to check the batteries regularly and replace them when they lose their charge.

Some units allow sensors to be placed so that the windows can be opened slightly for ventilation and still provide security.

Sensors are easily installed with screws or two-sided pressure tape. When the system is armed (on), the opening of a window or door separates the two matching magnets and the sensor transmits a signal—audible or silent—to the console, which sounds the alarm. If the signal from a sensor cannot reach the console, there are signal relays that plug into electrical outlets to send the signals through house current to the console.

Some sensors' audible "chirp" is heard every time a door or window is opened or closed, even when the system isn't armed.

A siren alarm for outside or the attic can also be added; an activated siren continues to sound if the console is damaged or disconnected by a burglar.

Add-on units are available to detect motion or sounds within one or more rooms or areas and to automatically dial a monitoring company or police when the alarm goes off. Another option is a module for wall plugs that will make a lamp flash in addition to the alarm sounding.

Hard-Wired Systems

Hard-wired systems connect sensors, control console, and keypads with actual wires, hidden in the attic, crawl space, or basement and the walls. The wires connect small, unseen sensors at doors and windows to the central console. All you usually see is the control key pad near the front door to arm and disarm the system.

Hard-wired systems are more permanent, but more complex to install than wireless systems. The hardware for a hard-wired system costs about half as much as for a wireless system, but professional installation costs about equal the hardware costs, bringing the total to about $1,200 for a three-bedroom, one-story house, with sensors at windows and doors, a motion detector, and monitoring equipment. Monthly monitoring charges are extra.

A "do-it-yourselfer" skilled in electrical wiring could install one of these systems. Many building contractors are wiring new homes for alarm systems.

With hard-wired systems, you don't have to worry about replacing batteries in each sensor, since there are none. A warning light lets you know when the console battery is getting low.

The control console, with a battery backup, is out of sight in a closet or cabinet. There is a small, relatively unnoticeable motion detector (usually infrared) within one or more rooms or areas. There is usually an alarm inside and outside. If a door or window is opened, magnet-activated sensors send messages to the control console, which sounds the alarm. Monitoring service by a commercial firm is usually included in such systems, at a monthly cost of $12 to $25. An option is flashing lamps if the alarm goes off.

When to Get a System

Plan ahead! Install a system long enough before you leave for vacation to give yourself enough time to get used to it and find out its quirks. You're sure to set the alarm off at least once or twice trying to leave or enter your place. And, find out what happens to the system in case of a power interruption or if someone turns off your power at the main control box.

Tell your neighbors or house sitter if you install an alarm system. If the alarm goes off, neighbors will wonder what can or should be done to respond. Some alarms can ring for hours, if unattended, although most communities have regulations limiting the length of time they can sound. Some units' alarms sound only 15 minutes at a time.

Shrubs and Trees

Take a good look at the outside of your house or apartment, even the second floor, if you have one. Dense shrubs and tall trees can hide windows from street view, providing a near-ideal place for burglars to work. Tree limbs can provide easy, quick access ladders to second-story windows. Prune shrubs and trees to eliminate these hazards. Some trellises for vines can also act as a ladder for second-story intruders.

Certain plants can be particularly useful in keeping burglars and Peeping Toms away from your windows. Shrubs and vines with prickly leaves or thorns can be incorporated into your landscaping, and many have attractive leaves, flowers, or berries. Some of the more common plants include barbary, holly, Oregon grape, pyracanthas, roses, yucca, and xylosma. Your landscape contractor or local plant supply or nursery can show you a wide selection to fit your climate and particular yard conditions.

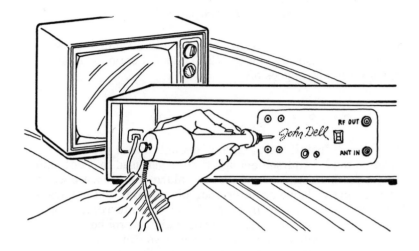

Valuables

Your sterling, silver service, cut glass, crystal, jewelry, and family heirlooms cannot be replaced, so you want to be sure they are protected while you are away. The following guidelines are useful whether you are going on vacation or not and should be part of your everyday life.

Mark Your Belongings

Your tools, bicycles, and appliances, such as VCRs, TVs, stereo equipment, portable radios, personal computer, printer, etc., can easily be marked with an electric engraving tool. On a spot that can't be easily removed, engrave your driver licence number and the state of issue. Do not use your Social Security number, because law enforcement agencies cannot receive any information based on Social Security numbers from the federal government. Marked items are harder to sell and easier to identify later if stolen.

Many local law enforcement agencies sponsor an "Operation Identification" program and can offer advice and assistance on

marking property. Some agencies will lend engraving tools to
local citizens upon request.

Inventory Your Valuables

All of your valuable items, especially those that cannot be
engraved, should be inventoried and photographed.
- Make a list of all your valuables. The list should be
  detailed so that the police or an insurance agent could
  identify the missing items and figure out their value.
  Some police departments, as part of the Neighborhood
  Watch Program (see "Everyday Protection Measures")
  will provide inventory forms for you to fill out, room by
  room, similar to those in the "Forms for Your House
  Book." You may wish to use a separate form for each
  room in your house.
- Photograph your valuables with color film or a video
  camera, particularly those items that cannot be marked
  with an engraving tool. Have your driver licence or
  driver licence number and state of issue on a separate
  card visible in the photo. Keep one set of photos or a
  videotape in your safe deposit box and one set at home.
- Key your photos to your list with numbers, letters, etc.
- If you have particularly valuable collections—coins,
  stamps, etc.—you may wish to consider a safe to hold
  them whenever you're not working with them. A display
  of rare coins in a home is easily taken by a burglar.

Storing Your Valuables

Unless your home is well protected while unattended or you
are leaving it in the care of a well-trusted individual, you may
want to store your valuables while your are away.
- You can put your valuable items in commercial storage.
  Check the storage area to be sure it is fireproof and
  waterproof, and that your insurance is up to date.
- You may want to put certain items in your safe deposit
  box (or rent one, if necessary).

- You can crate your valuable items and put them in an out-of-the-way corner of your attic, basement, or large closet. Even packing valuables away in a far corner of the basement is not always safe. One university couple packed their family silver, crystal, and porcelain—most dating back to the early 1800s—in a trunk piled with boxes with another stack of boxes in front. On their return from sabbatical a year later, everything was gone. They had left their home in the care of two trusted graduate students, who had to leave during the year and had sublet the home to some other students. Everyone denied any knowledge of the missing valuables on the couple's return. Nor did they ever find any parts of their priceless collections at local pawnshops.

If someone will be staying in your home, or at least checking in periodically, you may not wish to store things. But do not leave anything out that you treasure. Things can get broken in the most careful of households. You may wish to tell your house sitter to just not dust certain cabinets, shelves, or mantels rather than risk the loss of a Meissen figurine or Bohemian crystal vase. And you will want to let the sitter know which vases can be used.

Mail, Newspapers, Other Deliveries, and Bills

Whether you're at home or not, mail keeps coming, newspapers continue to be delivered, deliveries are made, and bills come due. Something needs to be done to take care of these matters when you are away.

Mail and Newspapers

Nothing says you're "not home" as much as newspapers and mail piling up around your front door or mailbox. The remedies are simple.

Mail

Unless you have a house sitter, you have several choices:
- Have a neighbor or friend pick up your mail daily at your mailbox. Many police departments recommend this procedure so that fewer people in the neighborhood will know you are away.

- Have your mail held at the post office while you are away.
- Have your mail temporarily forwarded to where you'll be.

United States Procedures

- To have your mail held at the post office, fill out an "Authorization to Hold Mail" card and file it at the local post office. There is usually a 30-day maximum on holding mail, but you can ask for a longer period. There is no charge to have your mail held.
- To have your mail temporarily forwarded, fill out a "Change of Address Order" (PS Form 3575), indicating the starting and ending dates. Note that only first-class mail will be forwarded unless you specifically agree to pay for other classes. The maximum time for forwarding under one request mail is one year. After the forwarding notice expires, mail is returned to the sender.

Canadian Procedures

To have your mail held at the post office or temporarily forwarded, fill out the "Request for Redirecting or Holding of Mail" card and pay the proper fee.

- The fee for holding mail at the post office is $2 a week.
- The fee for temporarily forwarding mail is $15 per three-month period (or portion). All classes of mail included.

Newspapers

You can have someone pick up your papers each day, or you can have them suspended while you are away. Some police departments recommend against suspending your papers, because then word can get around the neighborhood that you are away.

If you wish to suspend your paper, notify your paper carrier or the circulation office of the newspaper to suspend all deliveries while you are away. Call several days in advance of the last day you want delivery to let the carrier know what day you wish your final delivery and what day you wish the paper to begin again—and not to bill you for the absence. Then hope all goes well, although something is bound to go wrong.

You might wish to have the paper delivery stopped a couple of days before you leave, just to be sure the system works, and buy a copy each remaining day at a vending machine or news stand.

While you are away, have a neighbor or someone nearby watch for papers (and any flyers left at the door) that may be delivered after you leave.

For some reason, getting paper delivery started again can often be more difficult than having it stopped. Some newspapers have their systems so computerized that deliveries can begin only on a certain day of the week. If you want it on another day, you're out of luck; buy one at a vending machine or news stand. But a delay in restarting more than makes up for a stack of papers to read on your return—unless you really want all those old newspapers to browse through.

You can also cancel your subscription, and start a new subsciption when you return.

Other Deliveries

United Parcel Service, Canpar, Federal Express, and other deliveries must be thought about in advance. Whoever is watching your place will have to know in advance what you expect. Record your instructions in your House Book.

Bills

If you are going to be away for long, someone should check your mail for bills to be paid, checks to be deposited, and other items that need handling before your return.

Here are some suggestions for paying bills while on vacation:

- Have someone check your mail for bills as they come in and pay them with signed checks you have made out to the payees. If you don't know how much a particular bill will be, leave the amount blank to be filled in by the person paying your bills. Leave a list of the checks, by number and payee, so the amount can be recorded as the checks are mailed. You may have to leave some signed checks with no payee filled in for those unexpected bills, such as an annual insurance premium or a tax bill you forgot about.
- Prepay mortgages, charge accounts, loans, and utility bills. Call the payee in advance to see how this should be handled for each particular bill or account.
- Wait until you have returned to pay your bills and pay any late fees, if necessary. Some utility companies will, at your request, hold billing until you return; call in advance for details.
- Ask your bank if it can pay some of your bills while you are away (VISA, MasterCard, or some utility bills, for instance).

House Sitters

Why a House Sitter?

A house sitter stays in your home while you are away, caring for your house, plants, and pets, and performing other tasks that you may require. To decide if a house sitter is the best alternative to care for your home while you are away, consider the following:

- Do you feel comfortable with someone else living in your home?
- Does your house contain a lot of valuable things that you would feel comfortable leaving in the care of some one you may not know well?
- Do you have plants that need frequent care?
- Do you have pets that cannot be easily left at a boarding kennel?
- Do you have time to find and arrange for a house sitter you can trust?

If you have answered "yes" to some or all of these questions, then a house sitter may be your answer.

If you rent or lease, you must find out if having a house sitter will cause a problem with or the cancellation of your rental agreement or lease. This may be particularly important if you live in rent-controlled housing. If you live in a condominium or a cooperative, make sure that having a house sitter will not be inconsistent with the association rules.

Characteristics of a Good House Sitter

Here's what you will want to look for in a house sitter:
- *Honesty.* Do not let someone stay in your house if you're not confident that he or she is honest. For example, if a relative has a son who needs a place to stay, but the family has been aware that he has been involved in some shady dealings in the past, don't take a chance. You do not have to justify why you did not choose to let someone stay in your home.
- *Reliability and trustworthiness.* You should be able to count on your house sitter to carry out those tasks necessary to maintain the house, plants, garden, and pets. Avoid someone who has been or is involved in criminal activity, such as selling or using illegal drugs.
- *Maturity.* Choose a person who is mature and who will make good judgments. Age is not necessarily a measure of maturity. You don't want to come home and find that your house sitter was a party host who opened your house to any and all types of people in your absence.
- *Neatness.* Look for someone who is at least as neat as you are. If you have relaxed housekeeping standards then the person need not be a super neat person. On the other hand, if a neat and tidy house is very important to you, do not choose somebody who is a slob.

Your House Sitter as Your Key Contact Person

Your house sitter can be your key contact person. See the "Key Contact Person" chapter about choosing a key contact person. The main advantage is the ease of contact.

On the other hand, you may not feel close enough to the house sitter to want to ask him or her to take this responsibility.

This is a decision you will have to make depending on your particular circumstances and inclination.

Have Someone Check on Your House Sitter

It is probably a good idea to have a close friend or neighbor or your key contact person check in on your house sitter occasionally. You will gain peace of mind when somebody you know and trust keeps an eye on your home. Let the house sitter know that this person will drop by occasionally to see if the house sitter needs anything. The house sitter may also have questions that can be answered.

Your House Sitter and Your Car

If you let your house sitter use your car while you are away, you could find yourself liable for damages if your house sitter wrecks it, or kills or injures somebody, or injures himself or herself while driving it.

Sometimes, however, either because you trust and have known the person for a long time, or because of necessity, you may wish to let the house sitter use your automobile. If you choose to do this, there are several precautions you should take. See the "Vehicles" chapter for more details.

Be sure that your insurance covers the driver.

Obtain the driving record of the individual to be sure that his or her driving record is clean. In many states and provinces, driving records are a matter of public record, and is available to any other person upon request.

Include limitations on vehicle use in the house rules.

Spell out who is responsible for gas, maintenance, and repairs.

If the house sitter is involved in a car wreck, spell out the his or her responsibilities.

Finding a House Sitter

Finding a house sitter may not be as difficult as you may imagine at first. There are several sources.

Ask your friends and relatives if they know of someone who would like to house sit. Look for the young adult son or daughter of a friend who is in school and living at home. He or she may be looking for chance to be on his or her own for a while. A friend or relative may have a son or daughter who has just left the military or who is between jobs.

The parents of one of your neighbors may wish to visit your neighbor, but not like to impose on them; you may be able to arrange for them to stay at your house instead.

Call the student employment or placement services of your local college or university. They may be able to find a student looking for a house sitting job.

Call the house sitting services listed under "House Sitter Services" in the Yellow Pages of telephone books in many areas.

House Sitting Services

A house sitting service sends people into your home, either to live in or only to appear and take care of things on a daily basis. These services often employ senior citizens.

Before you hire a house sitting service, check it out. Ask for references; the service should be able to refer you to people who have used their service and are satisfied.

Ask if the service personnel are bonded; do not use a service that is not. Ask to see a copy of the bond and verify that the bond is in force. Find out the terms of the bond and who can claim against the bond.

Ask the service how complaints of damage or loss are handled. Make sure there are procedures in place and that they are understandable and easy to use.

Tell the house sitting service that you want to meet the individual who will be living in or caring for your home before you go away.

Find out in advance the cost of the service and the level of services performed. You don't want to get home and find out that watering the lawn was not included in the service.

Call the Better Business Bureau to find out if there have been any complaints lodged against the service. If so, find out how the complaints were resolved.

Make sure the service is concerned with your needs and concerns. Do not use them if they do not have fill-in forms asking for your requirements and needs.

House Sitter Selection—Like Interviewing Job Applicants

If you choose not to use a house sitter service, it will be necessary to select your own sitter. When selecting your house sitter, you are conducting a search for a valuable employee. Just as you would not hire an employee without an interview and checking references, do not hire a house sitter without doing the same. This applies even if you do not intend to pay wages to your house sitter. Your house and possessions are too valuable to entrust to chance.

The Application

Ask your potential house sitter to complete an application, such as the sample form located in the "Forms for Your House Book" at the end of this book. After you have hired your house sitter, keep a copy of the application form in a safe place.

The Interview

Interview your potential house sitter before making a decision to have him or her stay in your home. With the applicant, review the questions on the application form. Ask:
- What does the applicant think a house sitter's responsibilities should be? *Note:* You are looking for attitudes here. Whether the applicant has a good idea of a house sitter's tasks and duties may not be important. Good attitudes include a sense of responsibility, concern about your home and pets, and common sense. If the applicant conveys the impression that your home is a free place to stay without supervision, don't let the individual house sit.

- What are the applicant's financial expectations? Does he or she expect to get paid? If so, how much? Does he or she expect you to provide them with food? Who is going to pay for the telephone calls?
- How would the applicant handle an emergency? For example, what would do if the sitter came home and found that the house electricity was out or the toilet was backing up? You are looking for resourcefulness as well as common sense answers.
- Anything that you think will help you get an idea of the his or her honesty and reliability.

Prohibited Questions

Since this is like an offer of employment (especially if the sitters will be paid), there are several questions *not* to ask. These concern race, national origin or ethnic origin, religion, age, and, in general, other attributes not directly related to the job.

References

Check the applicant's references. When checking, ask the reference: How long he or she has known the applicant? What is the applicant's reputation for honesty and reliability? Is there is any reason why they believe that the applicant should not be a house sitter? Would they use the applicant to house sit their home if they went away?

Ask the applicant's former house sitting employers: How long were the employers gone? Did any problems arise that the house sitter had to deal with? If so, how was it handled? In what condition were the house, garden and pets when they returned from vacation? Did they get any complaints from the neighbors? Were they satisfied with the performance of the house sitter? Would they ask the applicant house sit again? If not, why not?

Evaluating Applicants

After you have interviewed all individuals and checked their references, think about how you feel about each one. If you have any reservations, don't choose that person. If you are married or living with someone, agree beforehand that if either one of you has reservations you will not use that person even if a "good" reason cannot be stated by the person who has the reservation.

Preparing Your House for a House Sitter

Prepare your house for the house sitter before he or she arrives. A few minutes of foresight and consideration now can save you money and help your house sitter do a better job.

- Set up accounts with your veterinarian, plumber, appliance repairman, etc. List these suppliers of services in your House Book.
- If your house sitter is not paying your bills such as water, gas, electricity, garbage, etc., prepay them or arrange to have the billing postponed. See the "Mail, Newspaper, Other Deliveries, and Bills" chapter.
- Clean your house. Nobody likes to move into a mess.
- Put your fragile items in a safe place, particularly if your house sitter has young children or pets.
- Child proof the house if your house sitter has young children. This means putting household cleaners and caustic substances out of the reach of children, and perhaps installing child proof devices on drawers and cupboards and protectors on electric outlets.
- Take steps to protect your valuables and heirlooms. See the "Valuables" chapter for details.
- Check your homeowners insurance. Does it cover damage the house sitter may do? Does it adequately cover you in case your house sitter or his or her guest is injured?
- Lock the doors to areas that are off limits to the house sitter. Remember, however, that if the heater, water heater, or pipes are in the basement or attic, do not lock the house sitter out.

Instructing Your House Sitter

When you have selected your house sitter and prepared your house, you need to think about leaving instructions. There are three types of instructions:

- Information instructions.
- House rules.
- Things to do.

All three sets of instructions should be spelled out in your House Book.

Information Instructions

Information instructions help your house sitter live in your house with a minimum of disruption. This is information that you take for granted because you live in the house every day. To an outsider, however, it may not be so obvious. The type of information to give includes:

- *Where things are:* dishes, flatware, cookware cleaning supplies, towels, sheets and linens, food, etc. Tell the house sitter what towels and sheets to use, what bed to sleep in, what food is available to use, etc.
- *How things work*: microwave, stove, oven, washing machine, dishwasher, etc. Put the operating manuals for the appliances in your House Book if they fit or in a convenient place and write the location of the manuals into your House Book.
- *The house itself:* where the faucets inside and outside are, where all the shut off-valves, circuit breakers or fuse boxes are and how to operate them. Include garbage pickup days, location of the nearest post office, and any other information of importance about the normal routine of the house.
- *The idiosyncrasies of the house:* does the hot water heater periodically rumble? Is it impossible to take a shower when the washing machine is on? Does using the washer and microwave at the same time blow a fuse or trip a circuit breaker?

- *Appliance repair firms:* plumber, gardener, handyman, veterinarian, pool firm, etc. List these names, addresses and telephone numbers in your House Book.
- *Telephones:* if there an answering machine, how does it work?
- *Alarm Systems:* how do they work?

House Rules

Your "house rules" are those things you don't want the house sitter to do or to use. Write the rules in your House Book, and go over them with the house sitter. Consider including the following items:

- *Wines, liquors or foods.* If there are some things in the house that you don't want the house sitter to use, list them and emphasize that they are not to be used. If there are foods, wines or liquors you do not want brought into the home, say so.
- *Entertaining.* If not allowed, say so. Outline your rules about guests of the house sitter. Discuss how many guests, whether they may stay over, etc.
- *Pets.* If you don't want the house sitter's pets at your house, spell this out.
- *Smoking.* If not allowed, tell the house sitter and tell the house sitter to inform his or her friends who visit.
- *Telephone.* Do you expect the house sitter to pay for all long-distance telephone calls? If you are in a message unit area, how many message units are going to be allowed as a reasonable use of the telephone? In some metropolitan areas, telephone use is charged by a measured time service within zones. If so, explain how the telephone is billed and what you will pay for, and what you won't pay for.
- *Subletting.* Can the house sitter sublet the house or let someone else stay if it becomes necessary for the house sitter to leave? You will need to have a plan thought out in case your house sitter becomes ill or for some other reason cannot stay.

- *Any other expectations or rules.* Write them out so that both you and the house sitter are clear about the rules before you go.

Things to Do

The "Things To Do" list. This list should spell out the things that you expect the house sitter to take care of while you are away. It could include the following:

1. Pets. See the "Pets" chapter.

2. Outside of the house. Yard, garden, etc. See the "Lawn and Garden" chapter.

3. Inside of the house. House plants, cleaning instructions, care of the mail, payment of bills, etc. See the "House Plants" and "Mail, Newspaper, Other Deliveries, and Bills" chapters.

4. Telephones. How is the telephone to be answered? What is to be said to people who call? Where are the messages to be written down? If there is a telephone answering machine, what is to be done with messages if the tape fills up?

5. Other. There may be unique or special tasks for the house sitter to do. For example, if you want letters mailed on the first of the month, write the instructions here.

Now That You Have Hired a House Sitter

When you have hired your house sitter, sit down with that person and go over the list of things to do, the house rules, and the information about the house. Explain use of the appliances and show how you how you want you pets, garden, house plants, etc. cared for. If the house sitter is a stranger to the neighborhood, introduce him or her to the neighbors. Show the person the neighborhood, the nearest stores, etc.

If the house sitter is to use the car, and have the house sitter drive it under your supervision.

Then get on with your packing, confident that you have made the best possible choice and that your house is in safe hands.

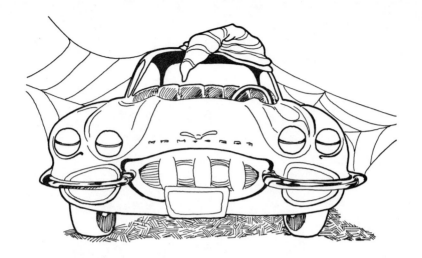

Vehicles

What to do with your car is less of a problem than what to do with your pet or garden. But the results of inadequate planning can lead to unpleasant, even disastrous and expensive, consequences.

Decide in advance just what you want to do with your car. You have several options. You can leave it locked at home, not to be used. You can leave it in the care of your house sitter, or you can leave it with a friend if you are concerned about the battery going dead.

Also, check your vehicle registration to see if it must be renewed in your absence. If so, contact the motor vehicles registration office for details on what to do.

Leaving Your Car at Home

You can leave the car in your driveway (locked), close enough to the garage doors so they can't be opened. But remember that a dusty car in a driveway is a signal that no one is using it and maybe no one is at home. If you leave it at home, particularly outside, be sure your key contact person has a key and the necessary information (model, make, year, color, license number) for police if the car is stolen.

If your car is not to be driven by anyone while you are gone, you can have your automobile insurance placed in suspense in your absence at a considerable saving in insurance premiums, because you pay only for comprehensive rather than your usual coverage. Check with your insurance agent.

Leaving Your Car in Someone's Care

If you decide that your sitter or a friend or relative will have the use of your car, take the following steps:

1. Be very specific on who can drive your car and whether a person with permission can let another person drive it.

2. Be sure that anyone you let drive your car is licensed.

3. Find out if that person's driving record is clean. Ask that person and verify it. You can often get any record (including your own) from the motor vehicles department for a small fee.

4. Check with your insurance company. Obtain claim forms and procedures to follow if the car is involved in a collision. Ask whether anyone except you can file an insurance claim for you in your absence, or whether they report to the insurance company and you make the claim when you return.

5. Make a detailed list of everyday and emergency information for your car, including the make, model, color, licence number, fuel requirements, details on insurance, your mechanic, and care of the car. See the "Forms for Your House Book" chapter.

6. Be specific about how your car is to be driven: only once a week to keep the battery charged or regularly. If you do not wish your car driven by someone besides you in rain, snow, or ice, say so. If there are limitations on how far the car can be driven and for what reasons, be equally specific.

As the car owner you are liable in case of injury or property damage involving your car, even if you aren't driving.

Car Alarms

If your car has an alarm, tell drivers how to turn it on and off, and what to do if it can't be turned off. Leave information for its repair.

House Plants

Your favorite ficus and philodendron can miss your loving care while you are on vacation. But there are ways to make sure they're alive and well when you return.

If Your Home is Unattended

If no one is staying in your home while you're gone, here are some tips:
- Repot from unglazed clay to plastic or glazed pots. Clay pots use up water about two to three times faster than plastic or grazed ones because they are porous.
- Move your plants out of direct sun, but not to areas that are too dark.
- Devise a watering system. There are several possibilities open to you.

1. Repot your plants into self-watering planters (about $10 each), which can hold up to three weeks of water. Before you invest in these planters, check with your local nursery or plant expert to be sure your particular types of plants adapt to this type of watering.

2. Use "water wicks," which water by capillary action. They can be made of nylon clothesline, glass fiber used for lamps, or thick cotton shoe laces, or even twisted nylon hosiery pieces. Put one end in the soil in the pot and the other in a raised container of water. Or remove the plant from the pot and put a wick up through a drainage hole and wind it around the inside bottom of the put; put some fine soil on the wick and replace the plant. Then put this pot above a container holding water, with the wick hanging down into the water. If you use one of these methods, try it out for a few days or a week before you leave to see how much water a potted plant drinks, and how long the reservoir can provide water to the plant.

3. Group plants in an artificial environment, such as a bath tub or shower enclosure, particularly one with non-direct light, and cover the top with plastic sheeting to make a temporary greenhouse to hold moisture. Water and mist plants well before leaving. Try to put plants with similar moisture needs together—cactus and african violets may not make a good combination.

4. Make a miniature greenhouse around a single plant with a plastic bag. Be sure the bottom of the pot is inside the bag, then seal it with tape. Keep it out of the sun, but in light; this should keep the plant moist for a couple of weeks.

5. Try a capillary watering mat, available at plant supply stores. One end of the mat goes into your sink partially filled with water. The mat is then draped up onto your counter top/drainboard, on which you set the plants, preferably in plastic pots. Someone may have to come in and check the water level in the sink while you're gone.

6. During warmer weather, set potted plants outdoors in a shaded, protected part of the garden, particularly if you have an automatic sprinkler, misting, or drip system to keep them from drying out. Do not move the plants abruptly from the warmer, more sheltered indoor location into a cooler outdoor environment, however. A few days before you leave, begin opening windows near them to get plants used to cooler outdoor temperatures gradually. It might help to put the plants in a shallow trench so they won't blow over while you're gone.

If Someone is Looking After Your Place

If you have someone who can come in and water your plants, again try to group them together—in the kitchen sink or a tub or shower—so watering can be easier and no plant is overlooked. Leave specific instructions as to how much and how often water should be applied. Tap water in some areas is high in calcium and other salts, which many house plants do not like. Water from most water softeners is high in sodium salt, which is not good for plants. If you do not use tap water, be sure to leave plenty of bottled water and notes on where more can be obtained.

Leave instructions, preferably in the House Book, for any fertilizer applications necessary, for sunning and misting schedules, and for any eccentricities a plant may have.

Even if you do have a house sitter, it is still a good idea to group plants for easier care, following the instructions you have left.

Lawn and Garden

Watering

For the beauty of your lawn and garden as well as the safety
of your property, have a yard sitter water and mow your lawns
and water your garden while you are away. A young person in
the neighborhood, a gardener, or a lawn-care professional can
do the job.

There are several things you can do to make watering easier
for anyone watching your home, or even take care of the water
needs for a few days if the yard is unattended.

Work out a watering plan so you will know just what you
need in the way of hoses, sprinklers, soakers, misters, and
timers, particularly if you do not have an automatic system.
Some plants and lawn areas may need more water than
others, so take this into account in working out your watering
plan. Times of day for optimum watering are also vital
information to include.

Some communities have watering schedules, and in some
areas watering is best done in the early morning hours to
reduce chances of water burn and mildew. Midday watering is
usually avoided.

Be sure details on the watering system are left in your House Book or a convenient place.

Water Timers

With various types of timers available, you can turn your sprinklers and hoses into an almost automated system that will work for short periods or help your yard sitter easily take care of the job. Timers fit between your outside faucets and hoses (or, less often, between hose ends and sprinklers) to shut off the water after a certain amount has flowed through.

Simple mechanical timers cost between $15 and $25, often less on sale, at hardware stores, plant nurseries, and discount stores. You turn on the faucet, turn the dial on the timer to deliver the amount of water you want or time for water to run, and walk away. The timer turns off by itself.

Computerized timers powered by batteries (about $30 to $45 at plant nurseries and garden supply stores) control faucets' off-on cycles during each 24-hour period. They can be programmed to turn the water on and off at the hours and minutes you wish on the days you decide, and are as easy to set as a digital wrist watch. The set program can be overridden if watering needs change (a rainy spell, for instance) by touching one control button.

Details for using the timers as well as the watering schedules should be left with your yard sitter.

Automatic Sprinkler Systems

If you have an automatic sprinkler system, be sure to plan for changes in watering needs of the garden seasons while you are away.

Some control panels can seem complicated and confusing. Be sure details for changing settings are in a handy place—in your House Book as well as on the inside cover of the door to the control box. Also, explain its workings to the person who will be taking care of your yard.

Drip Systems

A drip system, with or without misting capability, is an easy way to save water and to water specific plants or containers rather than a whole area. It can be one that is turned on and off manually or one that is part of your automatic sprinkler system. Drip kits with a variety of accessories are available from plant nurseries and supply houses and are not difficult to install. A basic kit costs about $14 to $25, depending on how many drippers there are. Misting kits that include a sprinkler and drippers cost about $25.

Moisture Meters

There are soil-moisture meter devices on the market that can signal an automatic or computerized watering system when the soil needs water.

Container Plants

Container and hanging plants on your deck, terrace, or patio and in your garden need special attention, even when you are home, so make sure these needs are met when you are away. Try to group your container plants for easier watering.

If you do not have a drip or misting system, a handy watering wand ($10 to $16) to reach higher plants and a watering can ($5 to $45 depending on whether made of plastic or metal) will be much appreciated by the person taking care of your garden.

Quick-release couplings ($1 to $3) for hoses and various types of nozzles and sprinklers are also a time-and-effort saver for you and your yard sitter.

Garden Care

Beyond just watering, there are other things that your garden will require while you are gone. The grass will probably have to be mowed, maybe even fertilized. In the fall, leaves will have to be raked up, and in the winter, snow may have to be shoveled. To keep flowers blooming, the faded blossoms need to be picked, and if you have fruit or vegetables ripening, someone should enjoy them in your absence.

Fill out the "Lawn & Garden Care Form" in your House Book for the person caring for your yard.

Pools and Spas

Pools and spas need care and security when you are away.

If you have a pool service, you should have few problems when leaving home for a while. If not, you will need to have someone watch over the system to be sure it stays clean and sparkling. Write out clear instructions. See the "Lawn & Garden Care Form" in the "Forms for Your House Book" on what to do if a pump or heater breaks down, and where chemicals are kept as well as where to buy more if needed. If you do not want anyone to use your pool or spa in your absence, make this very clear to anyone watching your place.

Check your fences, gates, locks, and lights to see that they are all in working order.

Pets

If you want to leave your pets behind when you go on vacation, you have several options:

- Board your pet at a kennel.
- Leave your pet with a willing friend, relative, or neighbor.
- Have someone come into your home to care for your pet.

The option you choose will depend upon the type of pet you have, its temperament and characteristics, and your temperament and concerns. Be realistic about your pet's personality when deciding. Board your pet at a kennel if:

- Your pet likes the company of other animals and people.
- Your pet has habits such as tearing up the furniture or urinating or defecating in inappropriate places.
- Your dog barks excessively when you are away.
- Your pet needs to be given medication.
- Your pet is not well trained and would be difficult for friends or house sitters to manage.

Out-Of-Home Care

Boarding Kennels

Selecting the right kennel for your pet can take time. Look at the kennels in your area and check their services and costs.

Remember, you are in charge, and it is your pet you're concerned about. You have the right to ask questions and receive satisfactory answers. Follow your intuition: if one kennel doesn't feel right, keep looking.

Where to Find a Boarding Kennel

There are several ways to find a kennel:
- Ask your friends and acquaintances where they have boarded their pets and their experiences, good and bad.
- Ask your veterinarian for recommendations. If your veterinarian runs a kennel, don't automatically assume that this is the best kennel for your pet.
- Look under "Dog and Cat Kennels" in the Yellow Pages of your telephone book.

What to Look for in a Kennel

There are no regulatory agencies in most areas that inspect kennels for safely and cleanliness. There is, however, a voluntary organization, the American Boarding Kennels Association, which has recently established a set of standards for boarding kennels. Association accreditation of boarding kennels is a long process and the number of kennels currently accredited by it is very few.

For information from the Association about its standards ($5) or a booklet "How to Select a Boarding Kennel" ($2), contact:

The American Boarding Kennel Association
4575 Galley Road #400A
Colorado Springs, Colorado 80915
Telephone (303) 591-1113

Many good boarding kennels operate more informally and may never be able to meet the stringent Association standards but may be perfectly acceptable for your pet.

Look at the area where your pet will be kept and ask questions about the care your pet will receive, such as:

Is the kennel clean? Don't expect perfection, but cleanliness—particularly the lack of feces or urine odor—is important.

Is water always available?

What type of food is provided for your pet? If your pet will eat only one type of food or requires a special diet, find out how will the kennel will assure that your pet is fed properly and if there will be an extra charge.

How long each day will your pet be in a cage or the sleeping area? Some pets—particularly cats—are happier in another area during the day, and often enjoy the company of people and other pets.

Will your pet be walked? Ask how often, how far, and how regularly.

Where will your pet sleep? Ask if your pet will sleep in a cage, alone or with other animals, whether there room for your pet to move around easily, and what will your pet sleep on. If your pet is to sleep in an area with animals, ask if there will be night supervision.

What does the kennel want to know about your pet? Be wary of the kennel that is not concerned about whether your pet has had its shots or does'nt ask about the pet's habits or problems.

Can you bring your pet's toys, bedding, and other items with your scent on them? You should be allowed to bring your pet's personal items.

What provisions are there for your pet's physical comfort? Check for shade in summer and shelter and warmth in winter.

What are the procedures if your pet gets sick or injured? Find out if the kennel will provide necessary veterinarian services by its veterinarian or yours, if there be a surcharge over and above the veterinarian's usual charges, and how much.

Does the kennel board sick pets? Ask if sick pets are separated from the healthy pets.

Do kennel personnel seemed concerned about the animals? Observe how they relate to the animals; if they show little or no concern for the pets in their care, try another kennel.

Does the boarding kennel handle pets other than cats or dog? If you have a more exotic pet, such as a bird or a snake, make sure the kennel is adequately equipped to handle it.

Costs

Rates at boarding kennels vary depending on your locality, and the particular kennel. Costs are usually on a per day basis. Make sure that you know the cost and agree to the terms before you leave your pet. Most kennels will require a deposit, at least.

Narrowing Your Decision

After you have decided on a kennel, ask the owner for references. If your are told that client names are confidential, suggest that some of the former clients call you. Avoid a kennel whose management is uncooperative.

Call the Better Business Bureau in your area to find out if there have been any complaints filed against the kennel. If so, check into the validity of and pattern to the complaints.

Contact the local health department or Society for the Prevention of Cruelty to Animals for any complaints filed against the kennel. If so, check into the matter further.

Make sure that the kennel has a business license if required by the local jurisdiction.

Picking Up Your Pet

Find out what the kennel's regular hours are and if you can pick up your pet outside these hours, on a weekend, or on a holiday. Ask what will happen if you are unable to return as originally scheduled, and if there be a surcharge and how much.

Boarding Your Pet With a Friend or Relative

Before you ask your mother or someone else to care for your pet, be sure this alternative is good for all concerned. You don't need your pet to strain good relations with your relatives or break up a friendship.

Some pets shouldn't ever be wished on friends or relatives. What you may find cute or even tolerable in your pet, your friends or relatives may not. Do not take a pet to another person's home if it is likely to tear the furniture, spray the walls, dig holes in the landscaped yard, or otherwise create havoc. Don't ask a friend or relative to board your pet if it bites, scratches people, or has habits that are either dangerous or upsetting.

If you think your pet is right for a relative or friend, is your friend or relative right for your pet? Many people are anxious to help their friends but may be unable to say that they really don't think they are able to keep your pet. They may not be aware of the responsibilities of keeping or caring for a pet. It is up to you to consider the problems that might develop and avoid them if possible.

Do not board your pet with friends or relatives if they:

- also have pets and all of the pets don't get along.
- do not have pets and don't like them.
- live in a radically different environment.
- won't be home on a regular basis.
- have a family and your pet is not used to being around people or children.

Instructing Your Pet's Caretaker

Write down instructions for feeding, exercising and companionship, toilet habits and needs, medication, special habits and characteristics, and general health and emergencies for your pet. Discuss these and your pet's special needs with your pet's caretaker. Read the section "Instructions for Pet Sitters" below for information necessary for your pet's caretaker.

Your pet should meet its caretaker before you leave to see that you are friends and can be trusted. If possible, leave your pet overnight at least once before you go.

Take the following items with your pet to the caretaker:

- Pet's customary food.
- Food dish and water dish.
- Medication.
- Bed or something to sleep on.
- Collar and leash.

- Identification tags and papers.
- Litter, litter pan, and pooper scooper.
- Pet toys.
- Release for veterinarian care, the name of your pet's veterinarian and instructions on what to do in the case of an emergency.
- Proof of your pet's vaccinations.
- Something with your smell on it.

In-Home Alternatives

Having someone come into your home may be best if your pet would find it very disturbing to be forced into a new environment. This is particularly true for cats.

There are two main in-home alternatives. The first is the house sitter. See the "House Sitters" chapter for details. The second is to have a friend, relative, or employee of a pet-sitting service drop in once or twice a day to care for your pet. The same person who cares for your house plants may also take care of your pet.

Before you decide to ask someone to come into your home to care for your pet, read "Why a House Sitter?" in the "House Sitters" chapter. Some people feel uncomfortable about other people being around or in their home when they are away.

Do not use a pet sitter if your pet:
- has habits that would be disturbing to a house sitter or other person coming in on a daily basis.
- is so strongly territorial that it will be aggressive with people other than you on the property.

Finding a Pet Sitter

There are several places you can look for pet sitters:
- Hire a house sitter. See the "House Sitters" chapter for sources, advantages and disadvantages of this alternative.
- Look in the Yellow Pages under "Pet Exercising and Feeding Services" for someone to come in on a regular basis.

- Ask your neighbors or friends or the responsible teenage children of your neighbors and friends.

Before deciding whom to use, consider the following:

- It is easier for people who live close to you to care for your pets rather than friends who live further away.
- Teenagers and retired people may have more time and be more inclined to spend time with your pet than will adults who are working.
- Persons who feed and exercise pets as an occupation may not be able to feed and care for your pet on the schedule your pet is used to, but may be more reliable.
- If possible, use someone you know rather than someone you don't know.
- If you use someone you don't know, make sure you get references. If professionals, be sure they are bonded and be sure to meet the caretaker before you go.

Instructions for Pet Sitters

Be sure your pet is well provided for. Tell your sitter any information that you know that will help the sitter care for your pet. Discuss and write out the following types of information:

Feeding. When, what, how much, where, to feed, how long food is available at one time, and any particular feeding ritual; specifically include what your pet is *not* to eat.

Exercise. Particular forms of exercise, regularity, and how long; walking routes; and special aspects to exercise or play.

Companionship. Type, frequency, length of time.

Toilet arrangements. Habits, schedule, facilities for emergencies; cleaning up after dog on walks; litter-box supplies, brand names, where purchased, and changing schedule.

Medication. Type, condition being treated, location, dosage, frequency, prohibitions in use, refills, side effects.

Special habits and characteristics. Runaway urges; obedience level; reaction to children, strangers, and other animals.

General health. Normal conditions, particularly those that may appear abnormal to a stranger; symptoms to watch for and what to do about them.

Emergencies. Specific procedures for illness and injury, including euthanasia, maximum cost of veterinary bills; written release authorizing veterinary services for your pet; name, address, and phone number of your veterinarian (arrange for the payment of any needed veterinary bill in your absence).

Death. Burial or disposal; your special plans or wishes.

Notification in Emergency

If you wish to be notified in case of an emergency, tell your friend or relative how to find you. See "Key Contact Person" and "Emergencies" chapters. Tell the pet sitter what to do if you cannot be found.

Introduce Your Pet to its Sitter

After you've chosen your sitter and written out your instructions, let your pet meet its sitter in your home. Let your pet know that this is a friendly person.

Consider the need to form contingency plans if your sitter is called away on his or her own emergency. Before you go, try to find a back up in case something goes wrong.

Make sure that your pet sitter has the name and telephone number of your key contact person. See the "Key Contact Person" chapter.

Other Animals

Dogs and cats are not the only pets that need to be cared for while you are away. Be sure to leave instructions for the care of your birds, fish, and any other pets you may have. The more exotic your pet, the more difficult it may be to find someone to care for it. Give very detailed instructions about its care and feeding to avoid unplanned problems.

Emergencies

You may not want to anticipate emergencies before starting out on a vacation, but prepare for them anyway. There are three kinds of emergencies to consider:
- Those involving your home or possessions.
- Those involving a friend or family member left behind.
- Those involving you while traveling.

In the first and second instances, you will need to decide what types of things you wish to be notified about, and how you are going to be found while you are away. In the third instance you will need to decide whom to notify at home.

Your Key Contact Person

Having a key contact person is the most important planning step you can take to deal with emergencies. Think of your key contact person as a liaison between you and your network of friends and relatives, since many don't know one another. See the "Key Contact Person" chapter.

First, if something happens to your home or belongings or to a friend or family member while you are away, your key contact person will be the one to contact you. Second, if something happens to you while you are traveling, your key contact person serves as a person to be contacted at home and determine what to do.

For example, if your mother becomes ill while you are away, your relatives can telephone your key contact person who will have your itinerary, possible contact points, and be able to find you. On the other hand, if you are in an accident and become unconscious while traveling, your key contact person will serve as an emergency contact person for the authorities. Your key contact person would have the necessary information to assist in your treatment, and would be responsible for notifying members of your family and others whom you designate.

Does your key contact person need to do more than just notify the appropriate person? For example, if your key contact person is your next door neighbor and you become seriously ill, you will need to decide in advance whom to notify—your parent, child, lover, or other individual. If you expect that your key contact person will do more than simply notify people, go over the plans with him or her before you leave and make sure the person is willing to do this for you.

Realize that the person may not do things exactly the same way that you would. But be grateful that it is done at all.

Kinds of Emergencies to Notify You About

You may or may not want to or be able to deal with emergencies that occur at home while you are away. Before you can decide, you need to:
- evaluate the types of emergencies that may occur.
- determine the feasibility of returning.
- develop alternatives to being notified.

Types of Emergencies

Emergencies can be divided into two types—those involving people and those involving things.
- People: Think about the important people in your life— spouse, an ex-spouse, children, grandchildren, parents, grandparents, brothers, sisters, nieces and nephews,

friends, and acquaintances. You feel closer to some of them than others. They can be in accidents, some serious, some less serious. They can become ill, they can die.

- Things: Think about what things you have—a house; a car; other types of investments such as rental property, stocks or bonds; or art, antiques, or collectables. Your house could burn down. The pipes could burst. Your home could be burglarized. There could be an earthquake, hurricane, flood, or other natural disaster. Someone could steal your car or it could be in an accident and be totally destroyed. It could get smashed just parked in the street. The stock market could go crazy. Your tenant's plumbing could go out. The roof could leak.

Make a note of any potential emergencies you might want or feel you need to come home for.

The types of emergencies you want to be notified about will depend on several factors.

Where are you going? Obviously, as you become more remote it will be harder to contact you. On the other hand if you are staying with relatives in another state, notification may be easier.

If you are far away and communications are difficult, expect to be notified only in the most serious of circumstances, if at all.

Are you willing to return home for the emergency? Sometimes it is not realistic to cut a vacation short to come home. You may not even want to know about an emergency at home if you:

- are visiting elderly relatives in a foreign country and you are not likely to not be able to go back there again while your relatives are alive.
- have purchased a non-refundable ticket in advance, are on a tight budget and cannot afford to get home, or are unable to come up with the necessary extra cash to return home early.
- could arrive only after the emergency is over or you couldn't help even if you could get home.

Contingency Planning

Before you leave, decide how to handle an emergency.

- Can the problem wait until you come home? What needs to be done now? Sometimes it is better to take care of the problem after your vacation is over.
- Can your key contact person handle the emergency for you? For emergencies that involve your things, your key contact person should be able to notify the plumber if pipes burst, or your insurance agent if the car is damaged or the house burglarized, or a repair person for an ailing appliance—note the repair services you prefer in your House Book.
- Can others handle the problem? Think about your network of friends and relatives. If you are the only person who is fully responsible in certain emergencies—your children still minors and live at home or you are an only child with parents who are dependent on you—you may wish to be notified. If you are a single unmarried adult with brothers and sisters at home who can deal with emergencies for you while you are away, you may not need to be notified. The greater your network of family and close friends who can be trusted to deal with problems that come up in your absence, the less you need to be notified about emergencies when you are on vacation.
- Can you assign a power of attorney to someone? If you know there are things likely to need your signature while you are gone, consider this option to take care of problems while you are gone. Before you do this, however, consult with an attorney concerning the associated risks.

True Emergencies

True emergencies are those you must be notified of and must return home to take care of yourself. They are not things that someone else can handle, things that can wait until you come home, or things you cannot get home in time to help do anything about.

How to Find You

Give the name, address, and home and work telephone numbers of your key contact person to your relatives and friends. Tell them the role you expect the key contact person to have in handling emergencies. Also, give your key contact person the name, address, and telephone numbers of all the significant people in your life, with their relationships or titles.

Develop an Itinerary

Your itinerary should be as complete as possible. If known, include places, dates, contact points, etc. If you are on an organized tour, make sure the name, address, and telephone numbers of the tour company are clearly stated. Give a copy of your itinerary to your key contact person.

If Not on a Set Timetable

If you are not traveling on a set schedule, you can do several things that can help you be located.

- Arrange to periodically telephone your key contact person at a set time and day of the week. This way, even though your exact whereabouts are not known, he or she will know when you are expected to call.
- Arrange to have general delivery letters sent to specified locations (post offices, hotels, American Express offices, etc.) on your route. This is not always foolproof, however, if mail is slow or not reliable in the country in which you are traveling.

Even if you do not always know your exact schedule, you sometimes have specific individuals you are going to call or visit along the way. Leave their names and telephone numbers with your key contact person.

Leave instructions with your key contact person about what to do if you cannot be found quickly.

If Something Happens to You While You Are Traveling

No one wants to think that something can happen to them while traveling. Those who think about it at all may feel that an emergency name and phone number in their wallet is sufficient. While this is a start in the right direction, you should consider something more.

Who Should be Contacted if an Emergency Happens to You?

In the event of serious illness or your death, you should have the name, address and telephone numbers—home and work—of your key contact person with you. At the top of the sheet, write "PERSON TO BE NOTIFIED IN CASE OF AN EMERGENCY." Make several copies. Put one in your wallet, one in each piece of luggage, and give one to your traveling companion(s).

If you are traveling in a foreign country, put one in your passport.

If You Die . . .

While it is not pleasant to think about, you can die at any time. Make sure you and your key contact person agree on the key contact person's role if this happens.

Discuss who is and is not to be let into your home in case of your death. Tell your key contact person whom to give the house key to.

Give your key contact person information about the location of funeral information, any burial arrangements you have already made, location of insurance policies, etc. Make sure he or she knows who will be responsible for making the necessary arrangements for services and disposition of your body, including organ donation.

Make a will or other plans for disposal of your possessions before you go. Make sure your key contact person knows where the information is located.

Afterward: Be Thankful

It is difficult to be calm in an emergency. But try to remember to be courteous to your key contact person in times of stress. He or she is doing the best job possible under the circumstances. Say "thank you."

Are You Ready to Leave?

As your departure approaches, you've taken care of newspaper and mail deliveries, arranged for your lawn and garden and indoor plants. If your home won't be lived in, prepare the inside, too. Use this checklist:

_____Unplug radios, television sets, and other appliances unless they are on timers while you're away.

_____Set timers and control systems to "on" (security, watering, etc.).

_____Prop open the door of your dishwasher to avoid mold growth from water or residual moisture. A small block of wood or plastic will usually do the job.

_____Stop mail, newspapers, and other regular deliveries.

_____Turn off water to the washing machine. This could prevent a soggy kitchen, utility room, garage, or basement floor.

_____In winter, in cold climates, drain the water system.

_____Check your heating/air conditioning so they won't use unneccessary energy heating or cooling your house.

_____Confirm pet, plant, and garden care arrangements.

_____Close fireplace flue so birds and other creatures won't drop in to visit.

_____Turn down the telephone bell so it won't ring and ring for anyone outside to hear.

_____Lock windows and sliding doors.

_____Leave necessary information in your House Book, and your itinerary, etc. in your house, with your key contact, or with a neighbor.

_____Make a copy of your travelers check numbers and (if you are leaving the country) photocopy of the first pages of your passport. Give them to your key contact person.

_____Notify neighbors, or apartment super or manager, and the police department.

_____Be sure the stove and oven are off.

_____Check to be sure bills are paid or prepaid (especially if you'll be gone more than a week or two).

_____Remember your tickets!

_____Remember your luggage.

_____Remember your wallet.

Forms for Your House Book

Contents

My Network

Relatives and friends to notify in case of an emergency

Name _____

Address _____

_____

Home telephone number _____

Work telephone number _____

Relationship _____

Name _____

Address _____

_____

Home telephone number _____

Work telephone number _____

Relationship _____

Name _____

Address _____

_____
Home telephone number _____
Work telephone number _____
Relationship _____

Name _____

Address _____

_____

Home telephone number _____

Work telephone number _____

Relationship _____.

Name _____

Address _____

_____

Home telephone number _____

Work telephone number _____

Relationship _____

Name _____

Address _____

_____

Home telephone number _____.

Work telephone number _____.

Relationship _____

Key Contact Person for _____

(fill in your name)

Key contact's name _____

Home address _____

_____

_____

Work address _____

_____

Home telephone number _____

Work telephone number_____

The Key Contact Person will be responsible for the following:
____ Emergencies: in case of an emergency at home, the key contact person will find us. If something happens to us, the key contact will tell others.
____ House drop in: The key contact will drop into the house from time to time to make sure everything is OK.
____ Other _____

Instructions for the Key Contact Person

Use this form for the information your key contact person needs to know.

If an emergency occurs to me, notify _____
Notify me if the following events occur _____

_____

_____

My itinerary _____

_____

_____

_____

Addresses and telephone numbers where I can be reached

_____

_____

_____

_____

_____

Additional items _____

_____

_____

If I die, the Key Contact will contact my network (see previous section)

Give key to the house to_____.

My will is located _____

Burial instructions are _____

_____

Other _____

Utilities Information

Electricity
Location of the service entry _____
Location of the main switch or circuit breaker, if different

_____

Where new fuses are kept _____

Electric company name _____

Workday service telephone number _____

Emergency telephone number _____

Gas
Location of the meter _____

Location of the main shut off valve _____

_____

Location of inside shut off valves _____

Location of the tools necessary to turn valve off _____

_____

Name of gas company or delivery service

_____

Workday telephone number _____

Emergency telephone number _____

Coal, fuel oil, propane delivery

When delivered _____

Location of chute or tank _____

Name of service _____.

Workday telephone number _____

Emergency telephone number _____

Special instructions _____

_____

Water

Location of the street valve or pump _____
Location of the main valve for the property or apartment

_____

Location(s) of the inside shut-off(s) _____

Location of the valve for draining the system _____

_____

Location of any tools necessary to shut off the valves

_____

Name of the water company _____

Location of the meter _____

Workday telephone number _____ .

Emergency telephone number _____

Sewer or Septic Tank
Location of the clean-out _____

Location of the septic tank _____
Name of company or plumber that you use to clean out pipes
or septic tank _____

Workday telephone number _____

Emergency telephone number _____

Garbage and Trash
Location of the garbage can _____

Garbage is picked up on _____

Location where picked up _____
It is/is not   necessary to move the garbage for pick up.

Items to be recycled _____

Recycled items are stored in _____

Recyclable items are disposed of by _____

Garden refuse is picked up on _____

Location where garden refuse is stored _____

Location where garden refuse is picked up _____
Company or department picking up trash and garbage

_____

Telephone number _____

Telephones

Location of telephones _____.
Location of telephone answering machine

_____.

How to start and stop the answering machine

_____.

How the telephone is to be answered

_____

What callers to be told about where you are and when you
will return _____

_____.

What is to be done with the answering machine tape when it
is full of messages _____
What types of telephone calls are to be returned

_____

Emergency telephone numbers

Police _____

Fire _____

Ambulance _____

Doctor _____

Non-emergency telephone numbers
Police _____

Fire _____

Key Contact Person _____

Appliances

All appliance manuals are stored at

_____

_____

Information and limitations on use _____

_____

Location of and how to use: dishwasher, washer, dryer,
toaster, oven, range, microwave oven, television, VCR,
stereo, other

_____

_____

Special information, such as inability to use certain
appliances at the same time due to electrical or other
problems

_____

_____

Appliances and procedures to care for floors, carpets,
windows, etc.

_____

_____

Heating, Cooling, and Water Softening

Heaters/Air Conditioning
Location of heating and air conditioning unit _____

_____
Location of thermostat(s) _____
There   is/isn't   a set back.
The unit is set back to ____ degrees at ____ o'clock and reset
to ____ degrees at _____ o'clock.
Turn unit on and off by _____

_____
Brand name and model number of the heaters/air
conditioners _____

Name of repair service _____

Telephone number _____

Water Heater(s) location _____

_____

Brand and model number _____

Name of repair company _____

Telephone number _____

Water softener
Location _____ When serviced _____

Name of service company _____

Telephone number for service _____

Lawn and Garden Care

Manual watering schedule
Front yard _____

Back yard _____

Container plants _____

Special areas _____
Automatic watering system
Location of instructions for water timers, automatic systems,
etc. _____

Mowing schedule _____

Fertilizing instructions _____

Leaf raking and show shoveling schedule _____

Flower, fruit, and vegetable picking instructions

_____

**Special instructions (bird feeders, animal feeders,
etc.)** _____

_____

Yard service (gardener) name

_____

Yard service telephone number

_____

House Plant Care

Location of plants _____

Watering schedule _____

_____

_____

Fertilizing schedule _____

_____

_____

Special needs of particular plants _____

_____

_____

_____

Type of water to use _____

Where to get the water _____

Other _____

_____

_____

_____

Pool and Spa

Cleaning instructions _____

_____

_____
Location of cleaning equipment and chemicals

_____

_____
Name of pool/spa service _____
When pool/spa service comes _____
Telephone number _____
Name of service person to call _____
Heater instructions _____
Filter instructions _____

Limits on use of pool/spa _____

_____

Neighborhood Watch

Neighborhood Watch contact name _____

Address _____ Telephone _____

Law enforcement agency contact name _____

Law enforcement agency telephone phone _____
Emergency law enforcement agency telephone number

_____

Mail, Newspapers, Other Deliveries, and Bills

Mail
____ Delivery continued
____ Forwarded to _____
____ Held at post office until _____
Post office telephone number _____

Newspapers
Name of paper _____
Carrier's phone _____
Delivery continued _____   cancelled _____
    suspended until _____
Name of paper _____
Carrier's phone _____
Delivery continued _____   cancelled _____
    suspended until _____

Other
Item _____   Phone _____
Delivery continued _____   cancelled _____
    suspended until _____

Bills to be Paid
Type _____ Check #_____ Amount _____
Type _____ Check #_____ Amount _____
Type _____ Check #_____ Amount _____
Type _____ Check #_____ Amount _____
Type _____ Check #_____ Amount _____
Type _____ Check #_____ Amount _____
Type _____ Check #_____ Amount _____
Special bill-paying instructions _____
_____
_____

Vehicles

The following information should be available to everyone using your car or other motor vehicle while you are away.

Vehicle: Make, model, year _____
License number _____ State or province _____
Location of operating manual _____
Location of files relating to the vehicle (warranties, repair records, tire and battery purchases, etc.) _____
_____
Limitations on use _____
_____
_____
Number of passengers allowed _____
Pets can/cannot ride in the car. Number of pets allowed ____
Type of fuel _____ Type of motor oil _____
The vehicle's eccentricities (how to start in the cold, how warm the engine runs in the summer, normal oil pressure reading, any strange knocks or noises you are aware of, etc.)
_____
_____
_____
_____
Alarm system details (demonstrate)_____
_____
_____
_____
_____

Washing the car: ____ Do not wash
Wash at home: where, how, what products to use _____
_____
At the following car wash _____
Other information _____

The following information should be available to everyone using your car or other motor vehicle while you are away.

Vehicle: Make, model, year _____
License number _____ State or province _____
Location of operating manual _____
Location of files relating to the vehicle (warranties, repair records, tire and battery purchases, etc.) _____

_____

Limitations on use _____

_____
_____

Number of passengers allowed _____
Pets can/cannot ride in the car. Number of pets allowed ____
Type of fuel _____ Type of motor oil _____
The vehicle's eccentricities (how to start in the cold, how warm the engine runs in the summer, normal oil pressure reading, any strange knocks or noises you are aware of, etc.)

_____
_____
_____
_____

Alarm system details (demonstrate)_____

_____
_____
_____
_____

Washing the car: ____ Do not wash
Wash at home: where, how, what products to use _____

_____

At the following car wash _____
Other information _____

_____

Car Insurance Information

Insurance company _____

Policy number _____

Insurance agent's name_____

Agent's address_____

_____

Agent's telephone number_____

Breakdown and Towing Information

Towing service you subscribe to (if you plan to drive while on vacation, you will need to keep the towing service number and plastic card for your own emergencies) _____

_____

Vehicle Repair Information

Mechanic's name _____

Mechanic's address _____

Mechanic's telephone number _____
Details on any service necessary while you are away

_____

_____

_____

Pets

Name/Kind _____

Description _____

____ Indoor   ____ Outdoor   _____ Both: schedule is ___

_____

Food: Brand and type _____

Where and when fed _____

Amount fed _____ Where stored _____

Where to buy more _____

Water: Where dish located _____

How often filled and changed _____

Special feeding instructions _____

Name/Kind _____

Description _____

____ Indoor   ____ Outdoor   _____ Both: schedule is ___

_____

Food: Brand and type _____

Where and when fed _____

Amount fed _____ Where stored _____

Where to buy more _____

Water: Where dish located _____

How often filled and changed _____

Special feeding instructions _____

Toilet Habits
Cats: Litter box is located _____

Fresh litter is _____

Clean box _____ Change litter _____

Litter-box liners are _____

Throw used litter _____

Brand and place to purchase litter _____

Dogs: Where and when to take dog _____

What to do if accident _____

_____

___ Pooper Scooper needed, is kept _____

___ Dog is curb trained   ___ Dog is outside dog only

Clean up by _____

_____

Exercise

Kind of exercise _____

Time(s) of day and place _____

How long _____ Leash is _____

Pet toys are _____

Medication for (name) _____

Type, when, and how to give _____

_____ Side effects _____

Emergency information
Name of veterinarian

_____

Address and telephone _____

_____

Arrangements for payment _____

Notify me if pet is injured or becomes ill ____ Yes   ____ No

I authorize $ _____ to be spent on veterinarian bills. If

above this amount _____

_____.

Burial instructions if pet dies _____

_____

Fish: Aquarium is located _____

Type of water and where bought _____

Food: type _____

Feed every _____ Kept _____

Costs _____, buy more at _____

Normal water temperature _____; to adjust heat_____

Special instructions _____

Birds: Type/name _____

Description _____

Special characteristics _____

Feeding: type of food _____

How often fed _____ Food is kept _____

Type(s) of food _____

Food is kept _____; buy more at _____

_____

Bird is/is not let out of cage. If is, when _____

Where _____ How long _____

Bird   is/is not   finger trained. Wings are/are not clipped.

House Rules

You may entertain a maximum of _____ guests between the hours of _____ and _____

Smoking (or no smoking) policy _____

Pets   are/aren't   allowed.

It is expected that you will pay for all long distance calls and all message unit calls that exceed _____ units.

Do not use the following _____ .
_____
_____
_____
_____

Subletting is not allowed.

Other rules _____
_____
_____
_____

Where Things Are

Linens _____
Flatware _____
Cookware _____
Cleaning supplies _____
Will _____
Burial instructions _____
Other _____
_____
_____

Your Valuables Inventory

Complete this form, but do not leave this in your House Book. Put it in a safe place where it can be retrieved if it is needed.

Items engraved with drivers license (VCR, stereo, TV, etc.)

Item	Make & Model #	Location

Cameras, sporting goods, portable items

Item	Make & Model/Serial Number	Location

_____

_____

_____

_____

_____

_____

_____

_____

_____

Power tools, mowers, etc.
Item   Make & Model/Serial Number   Location

_____

_____

_____

_____

_____

_____

_____

_____

Bicycles, motorcycles, motor scooters, snowmobiles, etc.

Item   Make & Model/Serial Number   Color   Location

_____

_____

_____

_____

_____

_____

_____

_____

Major appliances (refrigerator, dishwasher, washer, etc.)

Item   Make & Model   Serial Number   Location

_____

_____

_____

_____

_____

_____

_____

China & porcelain, silver, crystal & glass

Item	Number	Description	Location

Other items

Item	Model #	Description	Location

Insurance Information

List all your insurance information, except automobiles. It could include life, health, liability, homeowners or renters, boats or other special items, disability, and umbrella policies.

Homeowners' or renters' insurance

Company _____

Policy number _____

Agent's name, address, telephone _____

_____

Health insurance

Company _____

Policy number _____

Agent's name, address, telephone _____

_____

Life insurance

Company _____

Policy number _____

Agent's name, address, telephone _____

Other type of insurance _____

Company _____

Policy number _____

Agent's name, address, telephone _____

_____

_____

Other type of insurance _____

Company _____

Policy number _____

Agent's name, address, telephone _____

_____

_____

Other type of insurance _____

Company _____

Policy number _____

Agent's name, address, telephone _____

_____

Home Alarm Systems

Type of Alarm System: Brand and Model _____
_____ Wireless   ____ Whole House

Alarmed areas (where in house) _____

Windows & doors (which ones) _____

Location of console _____

How to turn on _____

How to turn off _____

Location of alarm operating instructions _____

_____

What to do if the alarm sounds _____

_____

_____

Name and telephone number of monitoring firm

_____

Code to use when calling or called by monitoring firm in

emergency _____

Name and telephone number of alarm repair firm

_____

Lighting Controls (Switches and Plugs)

Timed lights (locations, on/off times)

Front porch/yard _____

_____

Back porch/deck/yard _____

Living area _____

_____

Sleeping areas _____

_____

Other areas _____

_____

How to set or change controls _____

_____

Location of lighting controls instructions _____

_____

_____

_____

House Sitter Application

Applicant's name _____
Permanent address _____
_____

Mailing address, if different _____
_____

Drivers license number _____
State or province _____ Expiration date _____

Relative or friend most likely to know your whereabouts:
Name and relationship _____
Address _____
_____
Telephone number _____

Employer _____
Name of immediate supervisor _____
Address _____
_____
Telephone number _____

Vehicle make, year, license number _____
State or province where registered _____

Person to notify in case of death or illness
Name and relationship _____
Address _____
_____
Telephone number _____

Name and age of every person who will live with you while you house sit
Name and age _____
Relationship _____

Name and age _____

Relationship _____

Name and age _____

Relationship _____

Do you plan to bring any pets with you? _____

What type and how many? _____

References

Name and relationship _____

Address _____

_____

Telephone number _____

Name and relationship _____

Address _____

_____

Telephone number _____

Name, address, and telephone numbers of people for whom
you have been a house sitter _____

_____

_____

Short statement of why you think you would make a good
house sitter.

Do you drink alcohol? Yes   No

If so, how much per week? _____

Do you have any driving convictions (tickets)? Yes   No

For what? _____ When? _____

For what? _____ When? _____

Have you been convicted of any felony or misdemeanor
crimes? Yes No

For what? _____ When? _____

Odds and Ends

_____

_____

_____

_____

_____

_____

_____

_____

_____

_____

_____

_____

_____

_____

_____

Index

Order Form

We'll ship your order as soon as we receive it. We welcome checks, money orders, and Visa, MasterCards, Carte Bleu, and Access.

Thank you for your order!

Title	Unit Price	Total Price
Manston's Travel Key Europe	$10.95	_____
Manston's Travel Key Britain	$9.95	_____
Manston's Flea Markets of Britain	$9.95	_____
Manston's Flea Markets of France	$9.95	_____
Manston's Flea Markets of Germany	$9.95	_____
Manston's Before You Leave on Your Vacation	$5.95	_____
Californians please add sales tax		_____
Postage and handling		*included*
(Airmail outside U.S. please add $5.20 per book.)		_____
Total		$_____

If you pay by check or money order, please make it payable to *Travel Keys*.

If your check is not drawn on a U.S. bank, please send funds in your currency and add the equivalent of U.S. $4 to cover exchange costs.

Please do not send checks in U.S. dollars unless payable through a U.S. bank.

Over, please, for credit card orders and mailing address.

Credit Card Orders

We welcome Visa, MasterCard, Carte Bleu, and Access. Credit card orders may be placed by mail, or by telephoning 1- (916) 452-5200 day or night.

For credit card orders, we need:

Name of card holder:

Type of card:

Card number:

Expiration date:

Signature:

Date:

Ship this order to

Name:

Address:

City:

State or Province:

Zip or Post Code:

You daytime telephone number:

Send this order form to
Travel Keys Order Desk
P.O. Box 160691
Sacramento, California 95816 U.S.A.

About the Authors

Robert C. Bynum has been a public information officer, editor, and prolific writer for many years. He is also editor of most Travel Keys books. His own concern for his home, plants, and garden, and his interest in home security systems plus his attention to detail combine to your advantage in his clear explanations of systems, procedures, and hints for your own situation. His experience as a frequent traveler makes him well suited to help you plan your home's care while you're away.

Paula R. Mazuski, a California attorney, lives with her cats in a 70-year-old house in a busy downtown area. She travels frequently both for work and on vacation to various parts of the world. She combines her experience in preparing her home for her travels with her dedication and careful observation to help you make provisions for emergencies and get your pets, plants, cars, and home ready. Then you can have a pleasant and carefree vacation.

Bynum and Mazuski combined their own bits of information written on scraps of paper through the years, experiences in handling emergencies, and a rudimentary House Book with the extensive research and product testing that went into the making of this book.

About the Artist

Claudia R. Graham is a Northern California artist who delights in drawing children, animals, and Victorian houses.

Bon Voyage!